Empty-Nest Joyride

Empty-Nest Joyride

*Hope, Love, and Purpose
on the Road to Contentment*

LINDA HANSTRA

DEDICATION

To Tom, my steady companion on this journey.
Your love and support have sustained me on and off the trail.

Contents

A (Musical) Note to the Reader

What brings you joy?

I find joy—that deep sense of peace and contentment—in those I love, in the splendor of the natural world, and in beautiful music. Although my definition of "beautiful music" may differ from that of others', I'm sure most would agree that music touches the heart.

Throughout this book, I refer to song titles that have been meaningful to me on my journey. These songs may have played a key role in my relationships. They might depict a chapter in our lives as a couple or growing family. Or they simply keep me moving when I'm out on the bike trail. I have noted these favorites in bold print within the text, and indexed them in the endnotes.

Listening to music brings joy and energy that words on a page can't always convey. For this reason, I have compiled a playlist that accompanies the book. For added enjoyment, I encourage you to listen to these songs. The playlist is on Spotify (named Empty-Nest Joyride), and includes all songs listed in bold in the endnotes, as well as several more of our "empty nest" favorites. Enjoy!

Part I

A Bump in the Road

CHAPTER 1

The Road

My phone lights up with Tom's name, causing me to stop in my tracks. A text from my husband when he's out on his bike is typical. But a phone call? It halts my breath for a moment.

What's going on? Is it a flat tire or a broken spoke? Or has there been an accident? Is he the one calling, or has someone found him lying on the roadside and used his phone to call his emergency contact?

My thoughts are bordering on melodramatic, but after years of biking together, I've had plenty of time to imagine all sorts of scenarios. Pushing my grocery cart to the side of the aisle, I breathlessly answer, "Hello?"

As I await a response, the milliseconds seem like minutes. Predictability and routine have been the order of our days, but I have a feeling all of that is about to change.

My daily drive to work takes seven minutes. Less if I'm late, which is often the case, and more if there's snow, which—living in Michigan—is also often the case.

For eight years I've driven this way to the school, where I work as a speech-language pathologist to help students become better communicators. After working in another school district for several years, I'd jumped at the opportunity to work in Edwardsburg, where my four kids attended school. At first, they thought it would be strange seeing Mom in the hallways on their turf. But soon, they appreciated the security and convenience of having me nearby.

My car, affectionately named and tagged "KID MVR," made more trips from home to Edwardsburg than I could count. The kids preferred Mom's car to the school bus, so driving the KID MVR became my unpaid part-time job long before I worked in their school district.

Our weeks followed a predictable pattern. When Monday morning rolled around, the sleepy ride to school was a quiet one. By midweek, conversations on the logistics of evening practices, rehearsals, dinner, and pickup times filled the car. By Friday, everyone was chatty as we anticipated the weekend football games, dances, band competitions, and time spent with friends.

As the KID MVR pointed east each morning, we measured our year in sunrises. All September, the sun was already up as we hit the road. By October, our eyes feasted on pastel pink, orange, and purple skies that highlighted the fog nestled over the cornfields along the highway. Silhouettes of a barn or windmill against those colors made us fall in love with autumn all over again.

But in November, the pre-dawn darkness matched the black of my coffee and I let the kids listen to their jams on U-93—our local hit radio station. It wasn't until March that the glow of color finally reappeared. That's when we began our countdown to summer vacation. Just like us, even the seasons enjoyed a routine.

We're creatures of habit, and yet, when change occurs, we learn to adapt. My ride to work—and work itself—forever changed once that last kid left the nest in the fall of 2017.

Finally, I could listen to NPR in the car with no complaints, but I missed having "someone" to look for as I dodged students in the hallways. My kids had helped me feel young, connected, and needed; they'd been my security blanket as much as I'd been theirs. Now, the crowded school corridors concealed the loneliness I felt at school, at home, and in my car.

Although the car was quiet, the road was not. Michigan winters are hard on pavement, which alternately freezes, thaws, and refreezes amid frequent snow plowing for months on end. Eventually, U.S. 12, my route to and from school, became so disintegrated that the whole car shook and rattled as it rolled along, despite attempts to dodge as many potholes as possible.

When our county's road commission announced plans to repave U.S. 12 in Edwardsburg, the promise of this long-overdue construction project led to "woo-hoos!" and "yippies!" from parents, teachers, and bus drivers that echoed for miles around.

On that first teacher workday in August 2018, a year after Tom and I had emptied our nest, I couldn't miss the construction signs and bright orange cones lining the road. Pristine black asphalt stretched from shoulder to shoulder, still awaiting lane lines, but promising a quiet ride for years to come. As I approached the new pavement, I noticed an ominous warning sign: BUMP. I slowed to a snail's pace and gingerly drove over the uneven surface that connected the older road with the new. My car took the bump gracefully and then rolled with great anticipation onto the new pavement. I'm here to tell you: it was like butter!

Now I had a quiet car *and* a quiet road. I looked forward to the texts and phone calls of my young-adult kids on my afternoon drive home. The older two were off on their own, but the younger two were now in their fourth and second years of college.

"Mom, are you busy?"

"Mama, can I call you?"

I'd listen to their college-related problems that ranged from coordinating study-abroad travel plans to a pulled neck muscle that interfered with piano playing and conducting class. There was also the "I'm so stressed I think I need to drop a class" call. (*Do you realize that might mean summer school or, heaven forbid—a sixth year in college?*) and "I'm homesick. Can you help me pay for a flight home?"

I may not have been in their hallways anymore, but I was still in their lives, and they still needed me as much as I needed them to need me. Their calls reassured me my job as a parent was secure.

At the beginning of the year, I slowed down at the "bump" sign going east in the morning and slowed down again going west in the afternoon. It was reassuring to have the warning written in bold black letters on that bright orange sign, alerting me to the uneven pavement to come—letting me know I'd better slow down, take it easy, and get ready for an unexpected change in the road ahead.

If only life came with "BUMP" signs.

Tom's first words make me grab the grocery cart to steady myself: "I don't know what happened. I must have fallen. I don't know where I am. I think I broke my arm." Tossing the box of hamburgers back in the freezer, I leave my cart in the middle of the aisle and head toward the exit door.

CHAPTER 2

The Bump

It's a late summer Saturday, just a few short weeks before we are to drop Chloe off at college. Tom is out training for another century (100-mile) bike ride and I'm shivering in the frozen food aisle of the grocery store, comparing prices on hamburger patties and hot dogs to prepare for a picnic with friends that evening. We're cruising along on life's familiar path until 12:57 pm.

The phone rings, lighting up with Tom's name. Every time he calls me from a ride, my heart skips a beat even though the only bad news I've ever gotten is, "Hey, I have a flat tire. Can you come pick me up?" Still, there's the constant nagging worry that something bad could happen. The helmets and bright clothes we wear, and lights and reflective gear we use, don't always ensure safety. We know from watching the news and hearing tales from other cyclists that biking involves risks.

That's when Tom tells me about his fall. Attempting to hide the panic in my voice, I ask him a few questions. He repeats, "I must have fallen. I don't know what happened. I think I broke my arm. I don't know where I am." I hustle past the cashiers and out into the parking lot. After a couple more minutes of him repeating the same lines, I realize he is dazed and confused. I assume he has probably hit his head, maybe has a concussion, or worse—a full-on head injury.

Cycling wasn't a big part of my growing-up years. Shortly after learning to ride, I often wobbled down our steep gravel driveway to get my speed up, but it didn't always end well. I cried as Mom picked the dirt and gravel out of my bloody knees. Other than those early memories, I recall little about my childhood biking days.

My husband's formative years, however, included countless memories of riding bikes with his dad and two brothers alongside him. The foursome often ventured out on long, cross-country rides. One time, they made a several-day, nearly 200-mile trek from their house in Lafayette, Indiana, to his grandparents' home in Kalamazoo, Michigan.

His love for biking spilled over to me when we began dating. I wanted to spend time with him, so, since he was often on a bike, I joined in. After we were married, we spent warm summer evenings biking around town. We even took our bikes on mini-vacations to Mackinac Island, Lake Erie, and state parks in Indiana and Michigan.

After three years of marriage, in 1991, our family expanded with the addition of our first little one—a son named Jared—whom we took along on our rides. Two years later, we added boy number two, Seth. Though biking became more difficult, we continued with a Burley trailer and the boys in tow. Then four and six years later, the girls, Leah and Chloe, entered the scene. With four kids aged eight and under, the chaos meter was rising, and taking everyone out biking was like herding cats—not something one should do on a road with vehicles speeding by.

We put our biking lives on hold for several years. The bike seats grew dusty, the chains turned rusty, and the frames covered in cobwebs along the wall of the garage. We yearned to return to the freedom cycling afforded.

When Chloe, our youngest, turned sixteen and began driving herself, it was a milestone we'd looked forward to for some time. With extra time on our hands, Tom and I traded in the dusty and rusty bikes for shiny new road bikes and began riding regularly with a rekindled passion.

We hoped to ride even more when Chloe moved away to college and I mentally jotted down two empty-nest dreams: *Bike more. Write more.*

Until that point, my writing, along with the rest of my existence, had focused on the kids. I recorded their special moments and our parenting triumphs and struggles on a simple blog. Over time, I wrote more and more, filling my spare time at the keyboard. But as the kids began leaving home, I planned to shift the focus of my writing from the kids to long-awaited biking adventures for Tom and me as empty nesters.

We had been talking about our empty-nest plans for twenty-five years, starting after our first exhausting year of parenting. Of course, we loved the kids and our full house, but both often imagined more quiet and relaxing moments amid all the craziness.

Although we'd long dreamed of it, the reality of the impending transition with Chloe's graduation from high school sparked new discussions rooted in substance rather than imaginings. One conversation in particular stands out. It was as we drove home from church after the senior ceremony—the one where they showed all the seniors' pictures along with their college plans up on the big screen, gave each graduate a devotional book, and invited the parents and other church leaders to gather around them, lay hands on them, and pray. These young, bright souls were eager to embark on their new journeys.

"What are we going to do with ourselves?" I asked Tom as I gazed out the window, our church in the rear-view mirror. "With no kids around, what'll we talk about?"

"We'll talk about *us* for a change!" he said with confidence. "And our many biking adventures!"

I felt guilty for my recent lack of exercise. "I do hope I'll have more time for biking once this graduation open house is over and done with. Don't let me forget to order the mulch tomorrow. And are you going to take a day off to help me spread it?"

He agreed as I continued mentally stressing over my to-do list.

"Can you imagine this fall?" he said with a smile. "We're gonna have so much time!"

The thought simultaneously excited and terrified me as we rounded the curve of the country road leading to our home. We'd entered our woods, the trees of spring now so full we could no longer see through them.

Though we had no practice in empty-nesting and the path ahead was unfamiliar, we expected more time and unlimited freedom. Like that buttery-smooth asphalt on my road to school, we expected smooth sailing on the road to empty-nesting.

Instead, we experienced a big bump on that road, too.

Having worked in a rehab hospital my first years out of college, I'm all too familiar with the seriousness of head injuries. I know the brain can shut down quickly after an accident because of bleeding or swelling. I put those thoughts out of my mind and focus on the crisis at hand, on what I know rather than horrors imagined.

I encourage Tom to get his location from the biking app so I can come rescue him. But even with my explicit instructions, he can't figure out how to open the app, let alone read its map.

I know, depending on his injuries, seconds might matter. I hate to end our call as I picture him stranded and injured along some untraveled country road, but I finally say, "Honey, you need to call 911."

"Okay." But we're still connected.

I repeat myself, pausing after every couple of words for emphasis. "You need. To hang up. Your phone. And call. Nine. One. One." After a few more seconds, our call ends. He has figured out how to hang up. Before starting the car, I close my eyes and pray, "Please God! Help him remember how to dial 911!"

As I pull onto the highway, the congestion and craziness of Main Street add to the stress of the moment. I weave in and out of traffic, praying, "Please, God! Let him be okay!" Gripping the steering wheel, my wedding band digs into my ring finger, reminding me of the vows we took twenty-nine years earlier. We wrote them ourselves. We memorized them. And we promised to love each other "throughout life's trials and joys."

I call 911 and am forwarded to the dispatcher in our area, who thankfully says the other dispatcher is on the phone with Tom. They've located him and are sending out an ambulance. I'm given the location, but am also told if Tom needs to go to the hospital, they'll transport him.

I force myself to stay calm and mentally list the people I should call. I need to let them know there's been an accident, which will help keep my imagination from running wild while I drive to the site, which is a good forty minutes away.

Pushing aside a mental image of a bloody roadside and twisted bicycle, I call our daughter Leah, who will notify her siblings; then Tom's mom, who will call his siblings; then my oldest sister, who will let my side of the family know. The conversation is the same each time.

"Hello?"

My voice quavers as I tell what I know, which at this point isn't enough. "Hi. I'm trying not to panic here, but your dad/Tom had a bike accident."

"Oh no! Is he okay?"

"I don't know yet. He thought he might have a broken arm, but he was really confused..." I ask for prayers. Knowing people are praying reassures me. I know my husband is in God's hands.

I call the dispatcher again, who informs me the ambulance is taking Tom to the hospital.

"Do you know where his bike is?" I ask, knowing Tom would probably be more concerned about his bike—his baby—than his broken body.

"It'll be at the fire chief's house. You're welcome to pick it up there," the dispatcher says, giving me directions.

Minutes later, I pull into the driveway, and the chief steps outside to greet me. It's like I'm in a movie. After I introduce myself, he says, "Your husband's arm was in pretty bad shape and definitely broken." I hear the cars whizzing by on the highway behind me, but hang on to every bit of information the chief is telling me. "He has some pretty good road rash as well."

I anxiously ask, "Did he seem confused? Was he coherent?"

He places Tom's bike on the bike rack. "Yeah, he was a little confused." If it is a concussion, I pray it's a mild one.

Glancing at the bike, I notice some scratches, ripped handlebar tape, and a few other minor issues. Overall, it doesn't appear a car hit the bike (a constant fear of any biker), as the wheels and frame are straight and unbroken.

Relieved but still nervous, I lock the bike onto our bike rack, thank the chief, and head for the hospital. Another forty-minute drive. More phone calls. I suddenly remember we're supposed to host a picnic in a few hours. I call one of the guests, who will notify the rest of our friends that we've had to cancel the event.

Are plans beyond the picnic also in jeopardy? College move-ins are just around the corner. And after that, the joys of empty-nesting?

I notice detour signs ahead, but know I must keep moving toward my destination.

My thoughts are interrupted when my phone rings. It's Tom.

Much to my amusement (and fear), he springs the news on me as if for the first time. "I guess I had an accident on my bike."

"I know. You called me earlier."

"I did?" he says in disbelief.

"Yes. And then you called 911."

"I did?" He checks his "recent calls" list before he believes me. I'm relieved he knows how to use his phone again, but he has no recollection of either call. Again, I worry he may have a concussion, but for now, I'm satisfied to hear him talking and speaking clearly. He doesn't seem to be in great pain or suffering. He's calm and matter-of-fact, which is also reassuring. I wonder how far behind the ambulance I am as I pass by the fire station on Elm Road—the landmark we tell people to look for when they're coming to our house. Finally, I reach the ER and am led back to the small curtained-off room where I find my husband and survey the damage. Scrapes, blood, and gauze—lots of gauze. I see his scratched glasses and tattered bike shirt the medical team cut off of his body. He's pretty beat up, but is coherent and asking the doctor how long before he can bike again—a sign my husband is back to himself. He smiles at me, and I know everything is going to be okay.

After a few hours in the ER that had involved several x-rays, two CT scans, one preliminary elbow surgery (to clean it up and set it with an external fixator), and an echocardiogram (to make sure he didn't fall because of an unknown heart condition), they move him to a hospital room where he spends two nights. Before he's released, I'm trained on the daily cleaning of the pins that are drilled into his bones, holding his shattered elbow in place.

Besides caring for my now-debilitated husband, I focus on solving the mystery of what happened the day of the accident. Since he fell on his left arm but rides on the right side of the road, it doesn't seem likely he was hit by a car or clipped by a mirror, which would have sent him reeling to the right and out into the grass. He obviously fell into, not away from, the road.

After a couple of days at home, we revisit the crash site. I'm apprehensive. Will Tom have horrible flashbacks? I'm also afraid our discoveries will help me picture a scene I have no desire to play (and then replay many times over) in my mind.

Thanks to his biking app, we can pinpoint almost exactly where he fell. It's a country road with a decent shoulder. For bikers, that means no sharp drop-off. It's also a fairly smooth road—except in the spot where Tom had fallen. There, we see a common sight: a series of Michigan patched potholes across the right side of the road. Our first clue.

Even so, we both know riding over bumps this size, while leaving a bit of an impact on the tush, rarely causes a wipeout. How could these slight bumps in the road result in a serious fall, a crushed elbow, and shattered dreams?

Slowly, we piece together the events leading up to the fall.

"I remember everything up to about this point," Tom says, as he retraces his path. "I biked past this spot and saw the highway up ahead. I wanted to stay on the back roads, so I stopped, looked at the map on my phone, then turned around to go back the way I'd come from."

We replay the scene in our minds. Tom must have turned around and, before he was up to speed, hit the potholes. He also may have been putting his phone back into his bike bag and didn't see the bumps coming. Because he was moving slowly, his front tire likely got stuck and twisted in the pothole. Then *bump*—and boom! He was down. The weight of his slim, but tall, six-foot-three-inch body fell primarily on his left elbow as it hit the pavement.

Our brains have a way of protecting us from memories that might be too hard to relive. Since up to the present, there have been no further signs of concussion—for which I'm so thankful—we assume the confusion and memory loss at the time of the accident is due to shock. We accept the fact we may never know with certainty what caused him to fall. Still, I'm glad he doesn't recall the accident. It's painful enough for both of us to imagine. If he had to relive that scenario, the fear of a repeat might keep him from ever mounting his bike again and experiencing the joy of the ride that means so much to him.

CHAPTER 3

The (Re)Construction Zone

The next step on Tom's road to recovery is a visit to the orthopedic trauma surgeon. After looking at the x-ray of Tom's elbow, the physician's assistant asks, "What did you do? It looks like a mini grenade exploded in there!"

The injury is about as bad as they come and will require a five- to six-hour surgery to reconstruct the elbow, followed by another overnight stay in the hospital. On the way home, we drive past the University of Notre Dame, where Tom works as a system administrator for the library. Since he's been on medical leave for several days, we stop in to say hello to his coworkers and show off his new hardware.

The second surgery, to remove the external fixator and reconstruct the elbow, is scheduled for the day before our daughter, Leah, who is in her third year of school, moves into a new college. She's transferring schools and also changing her major for the second (and hopefully final) time. The following weekend, we plan a nine-hour drive to move Chloe—a first-year student—to her college in Minnesota. I imagine that long road ahead for both girls—their journeys into worlds unknown. Journeys much like the one Tom and I are on.

With Tom unable to drive and lift and haul boxes, the college move-ins require an alternative approach. Leah's school allows her to move in two days early, so Tom can ride along before his surgery, his arm propped up on pillows. Leah, Chloe, a friend, and I carry everything up two flights of stairs. We get Leah settled and say goodbye.

Tom's surgery the next day goes well, and the day after that, we enlist the help of our son Seth and daughter-in-law Maddie to "Dad-sit" while I run off to Leah's parent orientation meetings with my sister, who joins me for company and moral support. I'm spending more time in the driver's seat than usual.

The next weekend, we load up a small U-Haul trailer with the help of Chloe's boyfriend and we're on the road again. Although I prefer knitting and reading while in a vehicle, I discover I'm capable of driving for eight hours and Tom learns how to give up the wheel as he sits in the passenger seat with his arm propped up on pillows. Upon arrival, we're all thankful for those crews of juniors and seniors who assist the first-years on move-in day. As I help Chloe get settled into her room, Tom attends a few parent meetings to help ease his feeling of uselessness.

After a tearful goodbye, our baby girl sets off on her own and this old married couple, tired and broken, does the same. We still have two days to enjoy before I go back to work. As we rearrange our plans on the drive home, we focus on what we *can* do, rather than what we cannot.

I take the wheel again, driving south past Rochester and the Mayo Clinic, and then along the Mississippi River near LaCrosse, Wisconsin. It's dark and rainy, so we can't see the beauty we know normally adorns this road we've driven a few times before. Around the curves and over the hills, Tom controls the tunes. He turns on the sweet and romantic "Empty-Nest Playlist" he's been putting together in his now-plentiful spare time. I smile as I listen to the lyrics of "**Life is Better with You,**"[1] a reminder to cherish a love that endures through life's ups-and-downs.

With the kids officially out of the house, I retired my KID MVR license plate and logged onto Michigan.gov to try out some new ideas. I spent the good part of a day texting photos of the options out to the family for their input as to my new identity. I considered MT NEST, but the consensus was it looked too much like "Mount Nest." After several other options and much debate, I chose my new vanity plate: MTY NST.

I soon wondered, *do others read it as "empty nest" as I intended? Or do they see "mighty nest"?* I decided it didn't matter. For our empty nest was, indeed, becoming a mighty nest!

After twenty-six years of raising kids, Tom and I were suddenly alone together once again. But instead of taking afternoon bike jaunts and joining in the organized rides we'd signed up for that fall, we filled our calendar with doctor appointments, therapy visits, x-rays, and prescription pickups. After two weeks, the external hardware was finally gone from Tom's elbow, and the internal hardware—which looked like a mini Eiffel Tower on the x-ray—began fusing his broken bones back together.

Tom's arm was under reconstruction for several months, requiring many detours in our plans.

After eight weeks, he was allowed to drive again. Although the arm had regained strength and mobility, any slight vibration in the steering wheel bothered his nerves, sending shockwaves down his arm. A third surgery, six months after the accident, released the nerve from scar tissue, in hopes of eliminating constant pain and tingling in his left hand and fingers.

It seems impossible to believe now, but a couple of months later, he was back on his bike! Yet again, any roughness in the road running through the handlebars bothered his nerve. His doctors told him nerves take a long time to heal and so he waited. Every little tingle was the "thump" reminding us of where our old lives and dreams met a new reality, much like the bump on U.S. 12 on my drive to school. Even though the road crews eventually painted the lane lines, removed the signs, and smoothed out that one uneven spot, to this day, there remains a slight "thump" where the old road meets the new.

Our new reality isn't so bad. We have more freedom to do what we want when we want. We have more time for our own pursuits and pleasures. Our dinner conversations usually start out with a review of our daily events, followed by updates about the kids and what we may have heard from them throughout the course of the day.

I've kept up my writing because I still have some stories to tell. It's just that they aren't exactly the stories I originally thought I'd write about. But they're pretty good ones anyway: Stories of a couple of middle-aged empty-nesters, still deeply in love, still connected to their children, and—as promised some thirty years earlier—still together "throughout life's trials and joys."

We are still rolling down that road of life together, bumps and all.

TAKE FIVE! QUESTIONS FOR REFLECTION

A Bump in the Road

- Have you ever encountered an unexpected "bump in the road" in your life? Did this bump affect you only? Your spouse? Your children?

- If you've had a "bump in the road," how did you handle it? Did you learn any life lessons from it?

- What plans do you have for the near future? What plans for the more long-distance future? Have you considered the possibility of those plans not turning out the way you expect?

- What can you do to prepare for unexpected events that confound your plans and dash your hopes?

- What might God be trying to tell you about making plans and having expectations?

Part 2

Learning to Ride: Preparing for Life After the Kids Are Gone

CHAPTER 4

Winter Training

KEEPING THE SPARK ALIVE

It's mid-January, and on this cold winter day, I'm attempting to exercise. My core muscles scream as I struggle to hold a half-sit-up position. My legs quiver as I wake the muscles after their long winter's nap.

Back in October, when the weather got colder and the days shorter, I dropped most physical activity from my daily routine. Unless you count my shop-till-you-drop holiday preparations, or moving boxes of Christmas decorations up and down the basement steps, it's been roughly three months since I've physically exerted myself.

Every year I tell myself: *This is the year!* In those early days of January, I'm determined to continue my workout routine throughout the winter months, even though I can't get out and ride my bike. And every year, when the scale reminds me I ate too many holiday Oreo truffles and did nothing to counteract their damage, I tell myself: *Oh well, there's always next year.* My winter months' M.O. is to curl up in my oversized comfy chair under my warm fleece throw, and sip a cup of hot Lady Grey tea—all while holding my laptop, a book, my knitting, or the TV remote in my hands.

My body is at war with every ounce of my will. I know sitting in my big, comfy chair will not increase my life expectancy, nor will it prepare me for my first ride when the weather gets warm.

This year, as spring approached, I forced my body up out of the chair and into my workout clothes. I did that for about a week—without actually working out. Then, I put on my workout clothes *and* put "Yoga" on my to-do list. Surely this must count for something—like points toward a long life on some cosmic score sheet? Still, I fought the actual workout, and continued to enjoy my comfy chair, donned in my comfy workout clothes.

Today, overcome with guilt, I drove myself to the gym, where I sat in the car for another five or ten minutes, checking Facebook and listening to an NPR story about the latest government scandal. When I ran out of distractions and amusements, I dragged my sorry, out-of-shape body through the gym doors and began the slow, arduous process of stretching and strengthening these aging, flaccid muscles.

My winter training has begun. As I push myself through a yoga/strength fusion class, I avert my eyes from the in-shape bodies around me to whom I'm mentally comparing myself. I expect I'll feel sore the next day and tell myself, *no pain, no gain.*

I surprise myself by actually working out again before the week is up, this time hitting the treadmill and stationary bike. As I'm moving, I remember why I do this. Training is grueling, but it offers the immediate reward of endorphins pulsing through my brain, making my body happy once again! And even though I can't see it now, I know there will be an even bigger payoff on that first bike ride of the season. I'm glad to be out of my comfy chair, at least temporarily. This exercise thing does not come naturally to me.

In contrast, my husband seems as attached to his bike seat as I am to my comfy chair. Every fall, as the days get shorter and the air gets cooler, Tom rides for as long as he safely can. Eventually, the clocks fall back for daylight savings time and, while thankful for the extra hour of sleep, he immediately bemoans the fact that it'll now be too dark to ride in the evenings. Not to be deterred, he moves his bike to the basement, sets it up on the trainer, and without missing a beat, he continues riding three or four times a week.

Throughout November and December, I hear the whirring of his wheels accompanying his music or the TV while I sit and scroll social media or shop online for the kids' Christmas gifts. After a good hour, he reappears, all energized and dripping with sweat, as I shiver and pull my blanket more tightly around me. I shake my head from my comfy chair. We are definitely not made of the same stuff.

The saying goes, "birds of a feather flock together." But can two birds of different feathers build a *mighty nest* together?

We noticed our differences before we ever started dating. We were attending Purdue University and had joined the same student worship/fellowship group. Since we'd both grown up camping, we signed up for the group's outdoor weekend in late October.

That's when our differences first emerged. Tom's camping experience was a little rougher-and-tougher than the motorhome "glamping" of my childhood. That weekend, his hearty stock didn't mesh with my more delicate nature. Tom says I whined and complained about being cold all weekend. I recall little about him from that outdoor encounter.

Not long after that camping trip, I headed to the Student Union for my study break, where our fellowship friend group often met for an evening coffee. Call it luck or fate or God's perfect timing, but that evening, no one else from the group showed up except Tom. After some slightly awkward small talk, our chatting progressed into a genuine conversation.

Until this point, I'd paid little attention to this slightly geeky computer science major. But that night, while sipping our coffee during a much-needed study break, he listened while I poured out all the worries and fears about my studies. I was particularly concerned about a big thesis I was working on. Tom not only listened intently, but seemed to genuinely care.

"So, do you *have* to do this thesis?"

"Well, no," I said. "I can take the non-thesis route with comprehensive finals. But that seems like a copout."

"But if it's causing you this much stress, maybe you should drop it."

This was not sage advice. But having someone from my trusted friend group speak it out loud to me was all I needed to make the change. Within days, I dropped my thesis, and the stress dissipated like steam from a coffee.

Aside from the coffee chat, my memories of Tom from that fall are foggy. He was a nice guy, who, despite the need for a decent haircut and some updated glasses, was someone I *considered* inviting to the "Sadie Hawkins" dance at my dorm. In the end, I didn't invite him, but asked another guy instead, who—as it turned out—bored me to death.

Which got me to thinking about Tom again.

Then came December 16, 1986. Our friends planned a group outing to see that classic college-student movie hit of the '80s, *An American Tail*. (Yes, the animated film about a mouse. I know, we were a "wild and crazy" bunch!) We entered the dark theater and, either by luck or, more likely, unspoken intention, Tom and I sat next to each other. Between "There Are No Cats in America"[1] and the closing romantic theme song, **"Somewhere Out There,"**[2] our hands brushed together enough times to show us what we both wanted. When our fingers finally intertwined, we kept them there, sweaty palms and all, until the theater lights came up.

That's how it all began.

It didn't take us long to figure out, despite our differences, we were meant for each other. Tom was good at math, and I was good at music. But I also liked numbers, and he enjoyed making mixtapes—the "playlists" of the '80s. He'd grown up a city boy, and I was a country girl. But we were both Hoosiers and shared a common faith background. He was the oldest of four siblings; I was the middle of five. But each of us was rooted in loving families. And although his tent camping contrasted with my motorhome glamping, we both loved traveling and adventure.

We dated for only seven months before getting engaged. Nine months later, on April 16, we were married. Our mutual love of numbers made the date *4/16/88*—with all its multiples of four—stand out to us as a perfect wedding date. During those first sixteen months—while dating and engaged—and likely in every month of our marriage since then, we've learned something new about the way each of us ticks. We've argued and shouted; stomped and slammed; whined, complained, and cried. But we've also listened and compromised; learned and grown; made-up, hugged, and kissed.

During those initial sixteen months, I frequently asked Tom to assure me this was not a passing phase. I loved falling in love and never wanted to fall out of it.

"What if we lose our spark?" It was a question that had been on my mind ever since we started talking about marriage.

"We won't," he said with confidence.

"But I don't want to become one of those 'old' couples that live together and tolerate each other, but who don't seem to be in love anymore." Whether these "old" couples were actually unhappy together, or I just perceived them to be that way (since they'd likely learned to restrain their public displays of passion), didn't matter to me. Growing old and unhappy was one of my biggest fears in this whole thrilling, but unnerving, adventure of marriage.

He took my hand. "I promise you. We won't lose our spark. If we both want it and care for it, it won't go out."

Three years after we were married, when our son Jared was born, the chaos of our growing family followed. I'd never been busier and more exhausted than after becoming a mother. Then we had our second child, and I wondered, *how did I ever think I was busy with one kid?* And so on, and so on, through child number four. There wasn't much time for sleeping, let alone keeping the spark alive in our marriage, but we were determined.

We attended marriage classes and seminars whenever our church offered them. Delving into our relationship and taking the time to exercise our marriage muscles benefited us, sometimes in unexpected ways. We explored the differences in our upbringing, our communication styles, and our love languages. More importantly, we found similarities in our values, hopes, and dreams.

The classes encouraged date nights. This wasn't difficult, since the kids loved having babysitters, and we loved our couple time. The only sacrifice was a financial one. The added expense of a babysitter easily doubled the cost of a movie and dinner out. Still, a $75–$100 date night was a splurge we decided was worth it to keep our spark alive, even if it was only a handful of times a year.

Some of the best spark-igniters were the occasional kid-free getaways and vacations we took. We often spent a weekend in April celebrating our anniversary at a bed-and-breakfast near the shores of Lake Michigan. In 2005, when our kids were ages six through fourteen, a work conference for Tom allowed us to take a trip to Greece. We lined up grandmothers to care for the kids.

My mom stayed with the boys at our house. When she arrived, I rattled off my instructions.

"Okay Mom, here's the soccer practice and game schedule for Jared. He can tell you how to get to the soccer fields. Seth needs to practice his trumpet every day and remind him to turn in his practice record. I stocked the fridge with lunch foods and there are some meals in the—."

"Don't you think I know how to cook?" Mom inquired, looking at me with an *everything-is-going-to-be-just-fine*; *I-have-raised-five-kids* look.

The girls, who attended a different school and were on spring break, were carted off to Tom's parents with bags full of clothes, blankies, dolls, toys, books, and, of course, lists of instructions a mile long. Although she was too polite to give me "the look," I knew she was thinking the same thing my mom had as I pointed out the most crucial items.

All the packing and preparations were worth this adventure of a lifetime. We explored Athens and its surroundings, with its ancient temples, delectable food, and friendly people, before being ferried off to the romantic island of Santorini. It was a much-needed second honeymoon after seventeen years of marriage, and enough to reignite that spark once again. It was also a valuable reminder of the importance of caring for "us."

In the ensuing years, the kids continued to visit their grandparents for a few days each summer and went to youth group retreats in the winter, enabling Tom and me to enjoy kid-free time at home. It was rejuvenating! We could finally work on some projects around the house, have quiet dinners at our own table, talk without interruption, and light a fire from that spark. Even though the empty-nest years seemed far-off, we imagined a time when our lives would regularly be that quiet. It was an appealing dream for two tired and frazzled parents.

Despite my body's unwillingness, I manage to keep up my exercise routine and take a few short rides during some unseasonably warm spells that winter and on into spring. One of those early rides is on April 16, 2016: our twenty-eighth wedding anniversary.

The sun is shining, and it's a balmy seventy-six degrees. When we hit the road, I assume we'll take a lovely short ride. But once I get on my bike, I experience that surge of energy one gets when spring returns; my legs pump the pedals with power as the wind blows gently on my face. Thinking *nothing can stop me now*, I announce to Tom, "Hey, we should ride twenty-eight miles for our twenty-eight years of marriage!" Did I mention we like numbers?

He cocks his head and raises his eyebrows. "You sure you're up to it?"

"No. But I wanna try anyway. What could it hurt?" I respond, shrugging my shoulders in an all-too-confident manner. He hesitates but agrees, and so we head farther out of town.

After about fourteen miles, I question my decision. I'm not sure I can do another fourteen. We stop for a couple of quick breaks. The water, trail mix, and quick breather help, but only temporarily.

"Okay, so maybe twenty-eight miles is a bit far. Let's cut this corner and head toward home just in case I can't do it," I sheepishly suggest, hating to admit I'm not as conditioned for riding as I thought.

"No problem," he replies as he points us toward home.

Around the twenty-one-mile mark and still four miles from home, my legs and hips cramp up, and my energy quickly drains. In biker terms, I "bonk." I push through the next few grueling miles, but exhausted and utterly defeated, I have to quit after twenty-five miles.

"I can't do it," I say with regret. "What happened to me over the winter?"

"You just haven't trained enough yet, but you'll get there. You aren't ready for all of it at once," he encouraged.

"I guess twenty-five miles isn't so bad," I admit as my mind calculates the numbers. *I was pregnant four times during our marriage. Four times nine months is thirty-six months, which equals three years. Twenty-eight minus three is twenty-five.*

"Twenty-five is actually perfect," I said. "Since I was pregnant for three years of the twenty-eight we've been married, I shouldn't have to ride the last three, right?"

"Sure. Sounds fair. I can ride them for you. You go home and put your feet up." And with that, I biked up the driveway to our house, dragged my weary self inside, and crashed into my comfy chair. It never felt so good.

Regardless of how invigorated I was at the beginning, a twenty-eight-mile ride—much like a twenty-eight-year marriage—requires strategy, strength, and endurance. And that requires training.

As I look back on that day, at least three lessons emerge. First, I learn I need to get my butt out of the comfy chair long before a first ride of the season. The more time I spend stretching, strengthening, and doing aerobic activities over the winter, the more I'll enjoy that first outdoor ride.

Second, I must ease into biking in the spring. In recent years, my first ride is rarely anywhere except the easy, fairly flat, seven-mile loop through the country around our home. I add miles gradually until eventually, I can manage a "milestone" ride. I often try to bike my age in miles by the end of the summer, and I've been able to meet that goal several times.

Finally, I know it's okay if Tom and I achieve our biking targets in different ways. Since he rides his bike on the trainer all winter long, he doesn't require my gradual "warm-up" rides. After a few weeks of riding solo, we're able to take rides together. Thankfully, he doesn't mind going at a slower pace now and then, and I don't mind being pushed to go faster and harder to stay close behind him. It's a trade-off.

Just like a healthy marriage. Focusing on your spouse (and not just your kids) when you're younger is perfect training for the empty-nest years. Date nights, getaways, and kid-free time at home prepare you for being alone together again, once the kids have flown the nest.

Now, our days take on many forms: working on household chores and projects together, sitting in the family room near each other as we each do our own thing, planning our next vacation, and dreaming about retirement. We have all the private time in the world now, so there's no pressure to squeeze it all into one date night or kid-free weekend.

And that spark? It still burns.

In marriages, sometimes a spark will flicker and threaten to go out, but if you gently blow on it and care for it, it returns. At times, it's a glowing ember; the peaceful knowledge there's always at least one person who's got the other's back, who will push you to be your best, and who will wait for you to catch up when you fall behind. Other times, it's a full-on flame; a passion so deep that gale-force headwinds only make it burn brighter and torrential rains cannot put it out.

It's the spark of a love that can endure the triumphs and trials of two unique individuals who choose to take life's ride together.

TAKE FIVE! QUESTIONS FOR REFLECTION

Winter Training: Keeping the Spark Alive

- How have you prepared for the empty-nest season of life?

- What are your favorite "date night" ideas?

- Did you have any special "couple time" getaways as your kids were growing up?

- Are there any differences between you and your spouse that have become sticking points in your relationship?

- Are there any aspects of your marriage that need tending right now?

CHAPTER 5

Signals On and Off the Trail

COMMUNICATION SAVES LIVES. AND MARRIAGES.

I'm coasting down the hill and notice the distance between my front tire and Tom's rear one is shrinking.

"On your left!" I shout, and he moves over slightly to let me pass.

Now I'm in front. After a few minutes, I hear him shout, "Car back!" I edge closer to the shoulder and seconds later, hear the approaching car. It passes safely.

Ahead, I notice a spot of loose gravel. I drop and wave my hand, pointing to the gravel, to get Tom's attention and alert him to the hazard.

Approaching the corner, we both hold out our right arms to show we're turning.

The longer we bike, the better we become at signaling. It's a crucial part of a safe ride. Without good communication, accidents are bound to happen, so we've become adept at using several spoken and unspoken signals. But it wasn't always this way.

There was a memorable summer ride during our "half-full nest" years. The boys had moved on to college and were away on summer adventures. The girls, still in high school, had been attending summer marching band camp daily. Tom arrived home from work and, before asking how my day was, asked, "Are we going for a ride tonight?"

I weighed the pros—getting outside, spending time together, exercising; and cons—less time for chores and relaxation, having to change clothes. I glanced around the kitchen. There was no supper plan and the counter held its usual clutter. Then I noticed the papers.

"Oh dang! The girls forgot their forms, and they were due today!"

"Why don't we ride by school so we can drop them off?" Tom suggested.

With that, the pros overrode the cons, and I agreed.

We changed into our biking clothes, grabbed the forms, and set out. On the five-mile trek to school, we chatted about our day's accomplishments. The ride was smooth and exhilarating until we approached the school and turned the corner.

Band practice was nearly over, so the kids had moved inside, leaving the practice parking lot empty. I glanced at the new director's tower, which the administration had built earlier in the month. From the tower's vantage point, the directors could now see the band formations from above as the kids marched. When they spotted problems to be fixed, they could shout out directions over their megaphones and signal the stray marchers to get back in line.

"Check out the new director's tower," I said. Returning my gaze to the road, I screamed at what I saw ahead. The next few seconds seemed to unfold in slow motion. Yet there was nothing I could do to stop them.

Tom, who had been riding ahead of me slightly to my right, had turned left toward the tower, cutting me off. To avoid getting my front tire tangled up with his back one, I veered off to the right, lost my balance, and careened toward the pavement. In an act of self-preservation, my right hand reached out to break my fall.

A jolt shot through my shoulder like a knife. I also felt a burning sensation on my right leg and forearm where the pavement and gravel tore into my skin, rubbing it raw.

Tom, along with a woman who had witnessed the entire debacle from her front porch, raced to my side. Once we determined there were no broken bones, they helped me up to a sitting position in the grass.

"What happened?!" Tom asked, oblivious to the part he'd played in my fall.

We pieced together the series of poorly timed moves leading to my misfortune. When I'd said, "Check out the new director's tower," Tom turned to *go* check it out, assuming that I was turning to check it out, too. No signals. No warnings. Assumptions and poor communication had brought me down.

Two years into our empty-nest adventure, we had another crisis brought on by poor signals.

Chloe had taken a summer job at Grand Teton National Park in Wyoming. Our family vacation to visit her was the culmination of much planning and anticipation. I had dreams of peaceful and perfect hikes through the mountains overlooking lakes and waterfalls. My time with my husband and three of our adult children would be an opportunity to bring us closer together as we talked and laughed on the trails.

After a pleasant—but long—two-day road trip, we arrived! The mountains were more beautiful, the lakes more lovely, and the waterfalls more soothing than I'd imagined. But time spent with family? Let me just say, all my dreams did *not* come true.

It was wonderful to see each other after a long time apart. But when we got into the nitty-gritty of how we would spend our time, we quickly slipped into old habits. Personal agendas. Lack of patience. Difficulty expressing our wants and needs without resorting to manipulation and selfish demands.

On Sunday evening, as we planned out our first day of hiking, the kids excitedly talked about a nine-mile hike with a 2,000-foot ascent they were going to attempt. A hike that rigorous was out of the question for me. Tom, as usual, decided to stick by my side on an easier hike rather than run off with the young crowd. Still, he was miffed no one had even considered asking him to join the nine-mile hike. He loves a physical challenge, as well as competition, and would have been in his element. Fortunately, he was willing to sacrifice his own desires to be there for me.

On Monday morning, the kids headed toward the Delta Lake Trail, and Tom and I pointed ourselves toward String Lake with its four-mile hike and only 325-foot upward climb. Chloe, who was now familiar with the Tetons after working there all summer, told us it would be about a twenty-minute drive to the String Lake trailhead.

Unable to get a cellular signal for the GPS apps on our phones, we drove in the general direction of String Lake. When we came upon the exit from the National Park, it occurred to us something wasn't right.

"I have a signal now," I said to Tom as I looked at my phone. "Let me put it in Google Maps."

"Did I miss a turn? I don't see how I could have."

"Umm . . . it says we have thirty-nine minutes to go. I think we went the wrong way."

"Shit!" He pulled over to look at the map.

I pointed at my phone. "See. We were supposed to go here, next to the mountains. Instead, we're taking this road—all the way around these lakes."

"Great. We just wasted forty minutes of our vacation time driving."

If there's one thing I've learned about my husband after thirty years of marriage, it's that he doesn't like to waste anything. We eat leftovers. We reuse plastic bags. We get the most for our money.

And spending our vacation time driving when we should have been hiking was, in his mind, a waste. He was furious.

"We're not exactly *wasting* our vacation time," I said in my most calming voice. "We're spending time together, listening to pretty music, and taking in the scenery."

I convinced him to stop for some photos at a scenic lookout. The lake, framed by mountains above and pine trees on either side, was breathtaking. If we'd taken the shorter, easier route alongside the mountains, we would have missed what this longer, more tedious route provided. Tom forced a smile for the picture, but I could sense the tension below his pleasant facade.

One-lane-traffic because of road construction added more frustration, but we finally made it to String Lake. After a quick picnic lunch, we started our hike, walking single file. When the path was wide enough, we hiked side-by-side. Nevertheless, I couldn't help feeling a wide distance between us.

As I struggled up the trail, I paused several times to snap photos of the wildflowers and vistas of mountains and glacier-fed lakes. And to catch my breath. As I took in the picture-postcard views, I pondered God's hands that formed them. I captured the memories forever with my still shots.

Tom kept moving, finding his reward in the energy that pumped blood through his powerful muscles. He turned his GoPro video camera off and on as he walked, catching the action of the climb, the movement of the descent, and the flow of water down the mountain, over the rocks, and into the lake. He captured his memories in moving pictures.

It was another source of tension. I wanted to take pictures and saunter along. He wanted to move, move, move! I assumed he was wishing he'd gone with the kids for a more challenging hike, rather than being stuck dilly-dallying with me.

As we neared the end of the hike, our pent-up frustrations burst out as we argued about which route to take back to the car. I was tired and opted for the shortest one while he preferred to add another three miles to our hike. We were running out of time. I was adamant the longer route was not an option.

"I'm sorry I can't move as fast as you! I'm trying, but I have limitations."

"Oh, I'm well aware of your limitations," he said with a final air of disgust.

That hurt. More than the pain in my tired feet and aching legs, his comment cut to my heart. All the guilt of not having kept myself in shape over the years. The regret of not having worked harder to lose weight and get stronger before this trip. The hours spent in my chair instead of on my bike over the past months.

He immediately apologized. But he'd already released the words, and the damage was done. The apology was like slapping a bandage on a deep road rash.

We took the short route back to the car and only spoke of trivial things such as bathroom breaks, filling water bottles, and reconnecting with the kids for supper. We avoided speaking the truth—that we were both feeling frustrated, cheated, hurt, and angry. Astounding beauty surrounded us, but all we could focus on was ugly discontent.

We arrived at our predetermined meeting spot in time to have a late supper with the kids, who were also out of sorts. Their long hike had proved harder for some than others and had taken much longer than expected. With everyone's patience wearing thin, every minor grievance became another reason to snap at each other. What should have been a fun family time at an outdoor hootenanny—a party-like atmosphere with live, improvised mountain music and satisfying vittles—turned into gripe sessions about slow service and cold food. We finished eating and headed silently out to the car.

As we pulled into the parking spot next to our cabin, the arguing resumed. By that point, Tom and I had both lost our capacity for empathy. When he told me I should just "push through" my pain, I shot back, "Why do I have to listen to *you* complain about the nerve pain in your hand for two years, but you don't have to listen when I have actual pain?"

I regretted the words as soon as they were out of my mouth.

"How can you even compare my pain to yours?" he hollered as he slammed the car door and headed for the cabin.

I followed at his heels. "I wasn't comparing them! You know what I was trying to say!"

But did he know what I was trying to say? Did I even know what I was saying?

As usual, we yelled, then gave each other the silent treatment for a few minutes. Finally, Tom said, "What are we even arguing about?"

"I don't know. I think we're both just tired."

"Yeah. We need some sleep."

And so we kissed—our silent, cursory apology—and said "goodnight."

The rest of the vacation followed similarly. There were some memorable moments of love, laughter, and beauty, but they were mixed with tension, frustration, and regret. Once we started driving home with the familiar patterns of life in view, our emotions settled down. But the hurtful words and feelings we'd experienced continued to gnaw away at me.

Was it best to sweep these words under the rug and go on as if they'd never happened? Or should we uncover the deeper wounds they may have sprung from?

"I think we should talk," I said one evening at dinner.

"What's up?" he asked.

"I feel like we said some hurtful things on our trip. I know they hurt me. And they probably hurt you, too."

I explained the specifics, which had been spiraling in my mind. When I reminded him of that day when our signals were weak, he saw how he had hurt me and I also apologized for the role I had played. But I discovered he'd already moved on.

I broached the topic of seeing a counselor. He put his fork down and looked me in the eye.

"Do you think we're doing that bad?"

"Well . . . sometimes we're not doing that great. Lots of couples see a counselor to help them communicate better. I think we have a good relationship, but I wonder if counseling could make it even better. So we wouldn't blow up at each other like we did in the Tetons."

We talked some more, ultimately agreeing that if we repeated this pattern of behavior, we would seek help. Neither of us wanted to place our love—our most valuable asset—at risk. We were willing to protect it by whatever means necessary.

Over the next several weeks, we focused more on the other's well-being and gave each other more signals, both spoken and unspoken. One evening, I entered the kitchen and stopped in my tracks when I discovered a dozen red roses in a vase on the counter. The attached note read "Just because." Plunging my face into the velvety petals, I inhaled the sweetness of my favorite flower. They signaled the deeper, unspoken sentiment that, although we are not always on the same page, we will push through to our happy ending.

I sat there in the grass, the right side of my body throbbing as I waited for Tom. After ensuring I would be okay, he rode over to the school to give the girls their band forms and get the car they had taken to practice.

When he pulled up next to me, I tried to stand, but found I couldn't get up on my own. With the help of Tom and the nice bystander, I eased myself onto the front seat. The pain worsened as the initial numbness dissipated and the dirt and debris weaseled their way deeper into my skin.

We returned to the school to pick up the girls and drove home. I cleaned up the abrasions, took some pain meds, and surrounded myself with pillows and ice packs as Tom and the girls waited on me. When my shoulder pain didn't subside, I knew the injury was deeper than surface lacerations.

After a couple of doctor visits, an MRI, and finally surgery to repair what turned out to be a torn rotator cuff, plus weeks of intense and excruciating physical therapy, I felt better than I had been before the mishap! The old shoulder that—truth be told—had been giving me problems prior to the accident was now as good as new.

Sometimes, it's necessary to open a wound before the real healing can begin.

As a couple of old bike riders, we continue to value signaling, to communicate before making a move to prevent injury. We also know that even when our signals don't work and we end up sprawled out on the side of the road (or hurling insults at each other), we will remain to help and care for each other.

Once the hurt has healed and the pain subsides, we often end up better and stronger than before.

TAKE FIVE! QUESTIONS FOR REFLECTION

Signals On and Off the Trail: Communication Saves Lives. And Marriages.

- Recall a time when you and your spouse exchanged angry or hurtful words. How did you resolve (or not resolve) the issue?

- After an argument, do you tend to "sweep things under the rug" or take time to discuss your feelings?

- What signals can you give each other to let you know you're sorry, you're still in love, and you want to work things out?

- Are there any underlying issues in your relationship that might require professional help to resolve?

- What does the Bible say about love and marriage? (See 1 Corinthians 13, Ephesians 4:1–3, 32) How is God calling you to apply these words to your relationship today?

CHAPTER 6

The Rhythm of the Ride

KEEPING PACE WITH THE CHANGES

"**Y**ou got music?" a fellow biker asks as he passes me on the left.

"Yep! Keeps me going!" I shout, glancing down at my mini Bluetooth speaker that provides the rhythm I need to keep going.

Before starting out, I'd scrolled through my playlists. If it had been a Sunday afternoon, I'd have played my favorite praise song list. If I was going on a leisurely vacation ride on a Minnesota lake trail, I might choose "Quiet Biking" with its soft rock and acoustic songs.

But today, I want to keep moving. This is an organized ride and I want to finish somewhere other than last. So I find my "Lively Biking" list and hit play. The beat pulsates through my speaker and into my bones. Placing my feet on the pedals, I begin to pump. Down. Up. Down. Up. Down. Up. Down.

Not long into the ride, the blood is pumping through my veins as well. Once the adrenaline kicks in, there's no stopping me. At least not for a couple of hours. I have my tunes. I have my beats. I'm good to go!

The first song I hear is "**Good to Be Alive**",[1] and I know, indeed, it *is* good to be alive!

As my legs begin to burn and sweat drips from my forehead, I push ahead and pedal to the cadence of the song. Just as I'm losing steam, the next tune begins. This song—**"Home"**[2]—is more mellow, so I slow down a notch.

As the words filter through my brain, I picture *our* home—the place Tom and I have created together. It's our haven; our comfort zone. When we're there, we pedal to the same cadence. At least, that's the goal.

The first years of our marriage were a little rocky. It took us a while to find our rhythm and learn to balance each other's needs and strengths. We started with the "rules" we'd established at our pre-marriage workshop, when we divided up household chores.

"I like doing laundry, so I'll take that job," I said. "And since I'll be doing the cooking, I'm sure I'll usually get the groceries, too."

"I see myself handling the books," Tom said. "It's the man's job, right?"

Having both grown up in fairly traditional homes, this division of household tasks made sense to us. We muddled our way through marriage in our respective roles of working housewife and main breadwinner.

"When are you coming home? It seems like you're always working late," I whined over the telephone as six o'clock rolled around.

"My job comes with certain expectations," he countered. "If I don't put in the hours, I'm going to look bad. And that's not good for job security. Our security."

We settled into a rhythm. I learned his occasional late hours were good for us as a couple and the financial security of our future family. I knew what time to expect him. And he learned to call me if he was running late.

As newlyweds, our time at home was mostly quiet. We chatted about our days. We ate dinner. We watched "our shows." On Thursday nights, we ate frozen pizza and tuned into our favorite sitcoms: *The Cosby Show*,

Cheers, and *Seinfeld*. We lived, laughed, and loved in the stillness of our home. And in that stillness, we dreamed of someday filling our nest with the joyful sounds of little ones.

Eleven years and four children later, the atmosphere of our home was no longer serene. One evening, Tom walked through the door only to find me surrounded by two arguing kids, a whining toddler, and a screaming baby. Supper was late, and the kids were past cranky. I was, too.

"Can you help me?" I asked. "I was going to make spaghetti for supper and just realized we have no pasta!"

"If I'd known, I could have easily stopped by the store on the way home," he offered as we fumbled around the kitchen, coming up with a new menu of hot dogs and baked beans. It wasn't the first time.

I appreciated the sentiment, but it was too late to fix the craziness of the evening. We finally gathered at the table, bowed our heads, and asked God's blessing on our chaos.

Over time, Tom began to call before heading home to see if I needed anything from the store. Of course, if I'd truly developed a domestic rhythm, I might have had meals planned well in advance and gone grocery shopping once a week. But that's not the way I rolled. And thankfully, my husband rolled with me and rarely complained. Instead, he showed appreciation through his mealtime prayers, saying, "Thank you, Lord, for this meal, so lovingly prepared." The words sustained me during those early years of motherhood.

We also adjusted our rhythms regarding household chores. To this day, Tom empties the trash, mows the yard, and blows or rakes the leaves. I make the meals, plant the flowers, and weed the gardens. But we both help with dishes and indoor cleaning.

We found that the "divide and conquer" approach worked for us after learning our strengths didn't fit into all the traditional molds we'd once expected. I managed our social calendar, and surprisingly, our finances as well. Tom became the main laundryman and often brought home the groceries.

Our predictions of how we'd each contribute to the marriage had missed the mark. But once we discovered our strengths and learned to trust each other, we fell into a groove. Tom and I began to work in sync and the rhythm of the ride continued.

When our kids' school-age years were upon us, we found we could hardly keep pace with life's song. The parenting dance was so fast, we often lost the beat.

"How in the world are we supposed to get it all done?" I vented to Tom one night while we readied ourselves for bed. "The pediatrician appointments, dentists, optometrists, immunizations, orthodontists. Add to that the soccer practices, piano lessons, dance classes, taekwondo, and *homework*! Did you see how much homework the boys had tonight? And you know what's coming up, don't you?"

"Hmmm . . . February. Valentine's Day?" he guessed.

"No. I forgot all about that. It's the Science Fair I'm dreading. I'm going to lose my mind!"

The thought of developing hypotheses, procedures, experiments, trials, and those three-paneled boards was enough to bring on hives.

"I don't know how bigger families do it! I mean, I know some people think we're crazy for having four children, and maybe we are, but there are others with six or eight or ten kids! Now *that's* crazy!"

"I think you need to get some rest," Tom said with a quick goodnight kiss.

It was true. I was exhausted.

I survived that season, but as the kids got older, the homework became an even bigger burden. With college applications and entrance exams on the horizon, academics became a top priority. Our oldest replaced soccer with tennis and track. Piano lessons continued, along with flute, guitar, and voice. Dance classes morphed into high school musical rehearsals and marching band competitions. Youth group and the kids' burgeoning social lives rounded out our days. And nights. It was nearly round-the-clock busyness.

I yearned for the quiet evenings of our newlywed days.

Visions of an empty nest swirled in my mind. Did I long for my kids to fly away?

The fervor of our kids' lives filling ours grew steadily over the years. Those years were like the song **"Stairway to Heaven"**[3] by Led Zeppelin. It all starts out quiet as a newlywed couple, but then the tempo gradually increases until there's a house full of kids. As they turn into teenagers, the music gets louder with a fair amount of screaming.

The intensity grows to a fever pitch: screeching vocals, guitar riffs; loud and raucous.

And then, after a few measures, the vocals stop, the last guitar chord fades, and all is quiet. One voice breaks through the silence in a mournful but hopeful lyric—each syllable, each note, carrying the weight of the entire song.

With a suddenness we didn't expect, our bustling season ended. We felt the heaviness of that weight after we dropped Chloe off for her first year of college. In our now-empty nest, the music all but stopped. The demands and exhaustion, as well as the excitement and joy of children in our home, came to a screeching halt. All that remained were the memories.

How do you dance when there's no beat? How do you continue the ride when the music isn't there to push you along?

You keep on stepping just like you keep pushing your pedals when the music fades between songs. You can't stop in the middle of a ride. The goal is still out there and you need to reach for it, whether or not you can hear the music.

It was hard for me to do at first. I shed tears as I bid farewell to one phase of my parenting life forever gone. There was a palpable void in our home, our cars, and our routines. I discovered if I let myself focus on that void for too long, it became paralyzing.

But wasn't this the freedom Tom and I had longed for? Amid the chaos, hadn't we wished for silence?

My music pushes me to keep pedaling as I recall those "wonder years." The tune playing now is **"Verge"**[4] by Owl City, a fitting song for those final years with the kids at home. They were constantly "on the verge" of something big and momentous, like a performance, prom, or graduation.

Surely, I think, *our* new song can't be *all* bad. We search for and discover new possibilities. It's the two of us "on the *verge*" of something great!

Our evenings are mostly quiet now. Oh, there's a church meeting here, a show there. During the summer, there are bike rides before late suppers. Sipping wine and eating sushi on the back porch compensate for the nights when we still end up with hot dogs and baked beans.

During the winter, when darkness closes in, dinners of hot soup in the Instant Pot after a long day at work warm our bellies and our hearts. Books beg to be read. Yarn yearns to be knitted. Projects prompt us to work. Trips tempt us to plan. Writing calls me to sit and wrestle with words.

The household chores remain, but we find our balance. During the summer, when Tom hits the road for his long bike rides, I pick up the slack around the house. In the winter, he steps in to do more so I can find time to write alongside my regular job. We make it work. And when we do, we can hear the music—the joy in our everyday song.

Like Zac Brown's **"I Play the Road,"**[5] we're making our way home. Our crowd—our kids—have come and gone. They've left some emptiness, to be sure. But the silence now is so much richer and fuller than the silence we once knew.

Our home and our minds are full of memories. We recall events and special family times with fondness, and disregard those moments when we lost our rhythm—when the music turned to screaming and the drumming beat us down. Looking back, there's only one explanation for how we came through those times, still finding the rhythm and the song.

We had a Conductor who stopped us in the middle of the song to remind us we weren't playing for ourselves. Even though we weren't putting on a show for others to see, we had an audience.

Our Conductor himself is, as Big Daddy Weave sings, our "**Audience of One**."[6] Now when Tom and I sit at the dinner table, we join hands, bow our heads, and ask for a new start. Then we lift our eyes and look once again to the Conductor who shows us the beat, adjusts our tempo, and brings our song to life.

Take Five! Questions for Reflection

The Rhythm of the Ride: Keeping Pace with the Changes

- What tempo is your life moving to right now? A slow tempo? A fast one?

- Do you have difficulty balancing chores and work to be done in and around your home?

- How could you improve the current rhythm in your household?

- If you haven't entered the empty-nest years, what changes to the tempo are you looking forward to? Which ones are you dreading?

- If you are already an empty nester, has the change of pace been a good one? Or has it been harder than you expected?

CHAPTER 7

Rains, Chains, and Sags

THE PRACTICE OF REST AND RETREAT

We've been gearing up for this ride all summer.

Three years earlier, Tom had ridden his first 100-mile ride at the Apple Cider Century in Three Oaks, Michigan. He felt such a sense of accomplishment and pride that he aimed to ride at least one century every year for as long as possible. He was constrained to a "streak of one" the following two years, because of his accident. The nerve pain in his hand was still bothersome over bumpy roads and on extended rides, limiting the length of his outings.

But this year his injury is finally healing, and he's willing to suffer through the lingering pain in his hand and elbow to attain that 100-mile goal. His training starts at the beginning of the summer, with shorter rides on weeknights after work and one long ride on the weekends. Sometimes I join him and my distances gradually increase until I decide to register for the Apple Cider Century as well. I don't plan to ride 100 miles, but aim for a shorter, yet still challenging, distance.

When August and September roll around, our weekend calendar is full of organized rides, beginning with our annual Hospice Ride and ending with the Apple Cider Century—the crowning jewel!

Each organized ride brings a different vibe and experience. Michigan and Indiana countryside offer a variety of scenery and landscapes. Michigan has its rolling hills, vineyards, and orchards with ripe fruit on the vine and branch, and farmers sell the late-summer fare of tomatoes, peppers, pumpkins, and gourds at their roadside stands. Breaks between trees and beach homes afford us glimpses of the glorious Lake Michigan shore. Indiana's cornfields, a luscious green in July, turn golden and ready for harvest by late September. The Amish countryside brings us alongside pastures and stables for the horses we see clip-clopping down back roads, with black buggies and plain-clothed families in tow.

Besides the change in scenery, organized rides also offer cyclists a chance to interact with each other. Many ride to escape the big-city busyness of Chicago. Others drive from Ohio, Kentucky, Wisconsin, and beyond to join in the fun. Although bikers come in all shapes, sizes, genders, and ages, we've discovered the majority are in the fifty-plus category. Like us, it appears other empty nesters have found more time for riding after the kids have flown away. Retirees, who find even more time to ride, share stories of their biking and traveling adventures that make us green with envy, but mostly dreamy-eyed and hopeful as we plan our own future.

Perhaps the best part about organized rides, however, is that they offer something our own personal rides do not—SAG stops.

Most bikers are familiar with SAGs, but when I mention them in conversation with non-bikers, they ask, "What's a SAG?" and wonder where the word comes from. Some online sources say it's a rest stop for bicyclists who are beginning to "sag" or droop. It may also come from the French term "soutien au group," meaning "group support." But most English-speaking bikers I know use SAG as an acronym for Support and Gear, Support and Grub, or Sustenance and Gear. I prefer the latter.

The *gear* is what you might expect at a pit stop. You can get air in your tires, a little oil on your chain, or have some other simple mechanical problem fixed by ride organizers who supply whatever you might need. It's one less thing to worry about.

Tom and I also look forward to the *sustenance* at the stops. The variety of snacks and drinks available to replenish our strength and renew our commitment to finish what we've started varies by race.

Our annual Ride for Hospice offers healthy, unique appetizers from some of the best restaurants in town, while rides through Amish Country offer fresh blueberries, watermelon, and PB&J mini-sandwiches. Even better are the melt-in-your-mouth coffee cakes, donuts, homemade soft pretzels, and root beer floats that the Amish folk set up in their front yards. The Apple Cider Century—the ride we've anticipated all summer—offers, of course, hot and cold apple cider plus an assortment of energy-boosting snacks.

About a week before the Apple Cider Century, Tom checks the forecast and informs me, "Looks like it's going to be a great day! Not too hot, not too cold. No rain in the forecast."

Much to our chagrin, as the week goes on, the forecast changes.

By Saturday night, the eve of the ride, there's an 80–90 percent chance of showers all day long. But we've paid our fees and have been looking forward to this ride for weeks. There's no turning back.

In the morning, Tom and I, along with our son Seth, who is also hoping to ride a century, run from the car, through the rain to the Three Oaks Fire Station for the pre-ride pancake breakfast. My wimpy umbrella does little to keep me dry from the deluge. Since it's early—and still dark—I don't see the deep puddle until it's too late. Splash! My right shoe is soaked to the sock before the ride even starts. This is *not* how I'd imagined this day.

After breakfast, we hustle back to the car, taking on a bit more water through the clothes we now know are less-than-waterproof. The rain pounds on the car roof and blurs the windshield. We moan every time the sky lights up with lightning, and thunder rumbles off in the distance. We check the radar and forecast again and discover there's no clearing in sight, but it looks like the downpour might become a gentler rain if we wait a little longer.

After a few minutes, the sun rises somewhere behind the thick clouds and the rain eases some. The roads will still be wet, but hopefully the thunder and lightning have passed. Though not pleasant, our ride won't be downright dangerous.

We lift the bikes off the rack and wheel them over to the start line. Amongst other diehard riders, we mount our bikes and set off. The rain continues.

Tom and Seth plan to ride the full 100 miles. I'm not sure yet how many I'll ride, but I don't want to hold them back. We ride together for the first couple of miles, but then I watch them pull ahead and know I'm on my own. I listen to music and focus my mind on the long, arduous journey ahead. My initial goal: twenty-two miles to the first SAG stop.

That reprieve promises a mini-retreat on this long and challenging journey, similar to rejuvenating breaks one might take from daily routines—like time off work or a second honeymoon to rekindle the marriage flame.

It had been with this type of renewal in mind that I'd ventured out on my own mini-retreat just a few months before our organized ride season began.

The idea had emerged from one of my writers' groups when someone mentioned escaping for a couple of days on a personal writing retreat. *What a terrific idea!* I thought. I was juggling several writing projects and even though I was on summer vacation from my actual job, I was burning the candle on both ends with all the reading, writing, and learning on an ever-growing to-do list.

To my surprise and delight, the opportunity for a retreat came sooner than I expected, thanks to some friends of ours.

"We're heading out of town for a couple of weeks," they said during the fellowship hour after church. "You should go spend some time at our little cottage—we call it the Gnome Home. We love to share it with our friends!"

They didn't need to ask me twice. When Leah—who was home for the summer—and Tom granted me their blessing, I set my plan in motion. I was pumped and looking forward to a refreshing, productive getaway!

I arrived at the cottage Wednesday morning and took much of the day to settle in. Drifting back and forth from inside the cozy cottage to outside in the lush surroundings, I walked the grounds, sat on logs, and lounged in a rope-basket swing. I snapped photos of wildlife whenever they appeared.

But I wasn't doing much writing, nor even feeling very well. Perhaps the excitement (or anxiety) had messed up my digestive tract. The "blahs" hung with me all day.

I snuggled under the quilt that evening, hoping a good night's sleep would turn my mood around. I woke to the sound of a gentle rain, feeling refreshed and ready to work.

Until the guilt settled in.

Why did you go to all this trouble to pack and move out of your lovely home, with its comfy chair, screen porch, and beautiful backyard?

You have plenty of alone time at home, so was this necessary?

Isn't this a bit extravagant and self-indulgent? Who are you kidding?

The voices in my head continued as I stared out the window at the falling rain.

You're not special enough to deserve an entire cottage to yourself for two days. And at the rate you're working, you won't make a dent in your to-do list.

How much work is piling up on the home front?

One of my summer goals was to increase my use of spiritual practices such as meditating, praying, reading scripture, and fasting. If *reading* about spiritual practices counted, I was doing well. But, actually *practicing* spiritual practices? Well, not so much.

I willed myself to begin at that moment. Sitting by the window, where I could gaze out on the peaceful landscape, I started with meditation. . . and failed miserably.

I couldn't still my mind. *Get some writing done! That's why you're here!* It was all I heard when I tried to quiet my thoughts. My goal was to spend twenty minutes quieting my mind. It lasted for two.

To avoid more failed meditation, I opened up my laptop and searched for the definition of retreat. The first definition is a verb that means "an army drawing back from its enemy forces." In my case, that would be the forces of housework, other armies of distraction, and being captured by the sameness of my everyday experience. I could relate to those "enemy forces."

The second definition is a noun that means a "quiet or secluded place in which one can rest and relax." *If this isn't a quiet and secluded place, nothing is.* The evening before, I'd seen a doe and her fawn amble across the grass, completely unaware of my presence in the silence.

But I struggled with the "rest and relax" part. I had a mountain of work to be done, and a stack of books to read. I came on this retreat to work. But maybe I was missing the point.

Was it possible I was supposed to "retreat" in order to reflect? To meditate? Or pray?

Was this escape from daily responsibilities a gift to bring me closer to God? Was he giving me the permission to rest and relax that I wouldn't give myself?

In our media-filled, work-centered, goal-oriented lives, taking time to observe, listen, and open our hearts takes effort. And *practice*. Giving ourselves permission to practice these skills seems contradictory. We see practicing as a duty or discipline; not something to permit or allow, but to push ourselves to do.

Therein lies the problem. Our mindset has to change. Time spent reflecting and growing in the Spirit is a gift we can present to ourselves. If only we can give ourselves permission to accept it.

Can you give yourself permission to retreat? To accept the gift of time to reflect and renew your spirit? As these thoughts rolled through my mind, I listened to the rain falling drip by drip down the chain on the corner of the cottage.

I'd never seen a rain chain before. *What was it all about?* I Googled it until I found a picture matching what I saw on the corner of the cottage: a length of heavy chain from the roof to the ground, which allowed the rain to drip from link to link. The rain chain, Google told me, was an invention used for hundreds of years in Japanese culture. More aesthetically pleasing than a traditional gutter and downspout, the rain chain also serves a functional purpose. When rainwater hits the roof, the chain controls it, so it doesn't pour with a force that harms the foundation on which the house stands.

I watched as the rain chain slowed the gushing water, turning the steady stream into a pleasant waterfall. Each raindrop moved at an even pace from link to link, creating a lovely "plunking" sound on its way to the ground.

Like the rain chain, something (or some *One*) was telling me to take my time and enjoy the cozy cottage. To breathe in the fresh smell of the rain. To feast my eyes on the rich hues of green surrounding me. To quiet my soul.

I gave myself permission to slow down, reconnect my soul with its Creator, and leave the everyday responsibilities behind long enough to replenish my depleted resources. I readied my mind and heart for the work I was called to do.

I needed this retreat. It was a SAG stop on my journey. Not *Sustenance and Gear*, but *Solitude and God*. My heart needed this time of silence and closeness with God to both replenish my strength and renew the ambition to finish the work I started: Work that looks and sounds like rain on a rain chain as it falls with purpose and beauty—drip-drop, drip-drop—toward the foundation.

Though I could often benefit from such solitude with God, I'm not always in a position to get away for a retreat. So when I need inspiration and encouragement to keep going, I turn to God's Word, join a Bible study, or attend a church school class. As a couple, Tom and I check in with each other on spiritual matters, talking about our personal devotions or what good podcasts or sermons we've listened to online. We spend time together in God's word through mealtime devotions, small group Bible study, and weekly worship. The SAG of *Study and Guidance* moves us along on our spiritual journeys.

When we're going through something difficult, our friends, family, and church community have been there to carry us along. The SAG of *Support and Grace* holds us up when life is too much to handle on our own. With each passing year, we become more aware of our need for SAG stops of all kinds.

I continue to count down the miles to the first SAG stop. Imagining the hot apple cider that will lift the chill from my bones, I keep pushing the pedals. Down-up. Down-up. As a big hill approaches, I attempt to downshift. *Click-clack, pop!* My pedals stop abruptly. I can't move them. I brake cautiously on the wet pavement and come to a stop.

My bike chain, wet with the rain, has not only slipped off the gear, but has also become twisted and lodged in the derailleur. This does not look like an easy fix. Especially for someone who typically relies on her now-absent husband for all repairs. Glancing down the road behind me, I'm relieved to see two cyclists, a couple, coming up behind me.

They're approaching the big hill and it's clear they want to keep their speed up as they tackle it. As they buzz around me, I hesitate to slow them down or stop them. They yell, "everything okay?" and I shout back, "my chain fell off!" The woman repeats to the man, "Oh, her chain fell off!" and they immediately stop and turn around.

That's the great thing about bikers. We are strangers, but comrades on a mission together. If you stop to blow your nose along the side of the road, bikers passing by will ask if everything is okay. And if things aren't okay, as with my messed-up chain, even in the rain, they'll stop to help.

After a few minutes, I'm back in the saddle. The links of my chain are in place, securely fit into the gears. My pedals turn freely once again.

I'm thankful for the kind couple who stopped to help me out, since I'm back on track in a matter of minutes. I could have waited for a mobile SAG—a vehicle that drives around looking for bikers in distress on most organized rides—but it would have taken a while. It was comforting to know, though, that even if the friendly bikers had not come along to help me, the SAG wagon would have eventually found me.

I finally make it to that first SAG stop. As I take off my wet shoes and wring out my socks, I recall my frustration that morning after stepping in a puddle, and I chuckle. Both feet are now soaked to the skin. The old phrase, *into each life some rain must fall* (H.W. Longfellow) crosses my mind. It's certainly true on this day!

Life doesn't always bring sunshine. Struggles will come. The pressures of day-to-day life and expectations will pour down. The unexpected "slip of the chain" along my path might delay a goal.

But as I sip the hot cider and bite into a chocolate chip cookie, I trust I'll have everything I need—the sustenance and gear, solitude and God, study and guidance, and support and grace—to endure the rain that will inevitably fall.

Take Five! Questions for Reflection

Rains, Chains, and SAGs: The Practice of Rest and Retreat

- How do you make time for spiritual growth? What spiritual practices have been most effective for you?

- Have you ever been on a retreat that allowed you to get closer to God? If not, does this interest you? Why or why not?

- What support is available to you in your faith walk?

- How do you and your spouse "do faith" together?

- What "rain" is falling in your life? Where might you find relief from it?

Part 3

From Training Wheels to Taking Off: When Kids Become Adults

CHAPTER 8

Removing the Training Wheels

IT'S ALL ABOUT BALANCE

I hear the agonizing cries of my son from just beyond the mailbox. When I look up from my flowerbeds, I see Tom carrying Jared's bike, with the little guy hobbling alongside him. Gently taking his scraped-up hand, I guide him to the bathroom to clean up his bloody knee, dab on some triple-antibiotic ointment, and apply a Buzz Lightyear BAND-AID.

This is not the first time we've gone through these motions as he learns to ride his bike. But I wonder: *Is this the* best *way to teach kids to ride?*

Everyone knows you start them off with a tricycle. Then, when they're begging to be like the big kids on the block, you buy them a two-wheeler. With training wheels.

Those all-important training wheels make them feel like the big kids. At least for a while. But you know they can't use them forever. They'd look pretty silly riding around their college campus with training wheels. So you begin the exciting but dreaded task of removing them at an early age.

As a child, I experienced many falls, scrapes, and bloody knees as I learned to ride my bike on our gravel driveway. Falling was painful. But once the scabs healed enough for me to bend my knee again, I got back on. Trying and failing and trying again was part of the process of learning to ride. In fact, it's a process I've used repeatedly over a lifetime of learning new skills.

Tom, who had learned to bike at an early age, is excited to teach our kids to ride—the sooner the better. We initially take off Jared's training wheels as we hold on to the back of his seat, running behind to keep him upright while he pedals.

Finally, with a prayer under our breath, we let go of the seat. After two or three wobbly rotations of the pedals, he flops over, resulting in scrapes, bruises, and tears. We wait a few days for the fear to subside and try again.

We still aren't having much luck. So Tom asks a friend at work, who also has young kids, if he has any suggestions.

"I know the secret. Works every time!" his coworker says.

Tom listens as he explains the key. "The kid needs to learn balance before he can add the complication of pedaling. Once they understand balance, the rest is a piece of cake!"

"How do you teach them that?" Tom asks, imagining a complicated set of exercises or balance beams in the basement.

"You take off the pedals! Let your boy put his feet on the ground and push himself for a few feet. Once he gets rolling, have him pick his feet up. When he wobbles, he'll catch himself with his feet."

"Then what?" This method intrigues Tom.

"He lifts his feet again. Each time, he rolls a little farther and balances a little longer. He wobbles—catches himself—rolls some more. Before you know it, he'll only put his feet down to push himself along faster."

"Sounds good so far. No falling and no fear. I like it. Then what?"

"Then you put the pedals back on and he'll fly! Try it. It'll amaze you!" Tom's friend leans back in his chair and smiles, almost daring Tom to prove him wrong.

That evening, Tom gets to work on the pedals. "What are you doing to my bike, Dad?" Jared asks.

"You'll see."

The new technique works! Jared wobbles a little, but quickly catches himself as he learns the art of balancing. Within a few minutes, Tom replaces the pedals. We can't believe how easily his little feet spin around. He's on his way!

Each of our four kids learned to ride a bike that way, and the method is now mainstream with the innovation of "balance bikes." Low to the ground with no pedals, toddlers as young as a year old learn to ride on them.

When our kids matured into young adults leaving home, the pattern repeated itself. They learned balance first. Then they added more skill. Finally, they were independent.

As Tom and I let go of each of them—watching all four stumble and soar from their teenage years into adulthood—we saw the importance of balance once again. They learned to balance work and play, studies and social life, spending and saving, moving on and staying put.

As parents, we also learned balance—the art of knowing when to step in and when to let go. We teetered between protecting them from danger and preventing them from pursuing their dreams. They wobbled at times, but knew, when they needed the solid ground of our support, they could just reach out and find it.

Like watching them conquer riding a two-wheeler, we walked that fine line between holding on and letting go.

Take Five! Questions for Reflection

Removing the Training Wheels: It's All About Balance

- What aspects of the empty nest have you had difficulty balancing?

- What is the difference between helping and enabling your adult child?

- How can you show interest in your children's lives without interfering?

- How do you know when to let go of your child's hand?

- Are there times you should step in and help out?

CHAPTER 9

Rivers and Rollers

JARED'S STORY

"**B**e careful! Those stones are super slippery!" I shout a second too late, as I watch the first of my kids slip onto his butt and into the water. Jared—his shorts now drenched—laughs as he gingerly steps back onto the rocks just in time to catch his sister who's next to slip-slide off.

We're visiting Itasca State Park—one of our favorite spots in Northern Minnesota. The word "Itasca" comes from the Latin "VerITAS CAput," or "true head." It's the "true head" of the Mississippi River.

We've walk across those slippery stones many times as we cross the twenty-foot span of water, only inches deep and flowing at an average of six cubic feet—or forty-five gallons—per second. But the mighty Mississippi grows as it goes.

It passes through lakes and joins other small tributaries until it reaches Minneapolis/St. Paul, where its rate increases to 12,000 cubic feet—now 90,000 gallons—per second. By the time it reaches the Gulf of Mexico at the mouth of the river, it can span three miles and carries 600,000 cubic feet of water per second at depths as great as 200 feet.

We often visit the slippery stones of the river's head to cool off after biking the seventeen-mile paved trail that encircles the park.

The trail isn't too difficult, but it's a great workout because it's full of "rollers," a series of small and medium-sized hills. Going up the first hill takes some energy, but when you crest it, you can coast on the downward slope, get your speed up, and tackle the next rise with momentum.

I squeal with delight as I glide down the hills, and enjoy the gorgeous scenery of Northern Minnesota. The rise and fall of these rollers reminds me of roller coasters and our own "roller-coaster boy."

It was a few weeks before Christmas, 2003. As one did back then, I'd been browsing through catalogs and sales flyers to make my annual shopping list. My oldest, Jared, peered over my shoulder.

"Mom?"

"Yes?" The look on his twelve-year-old face told me he was either dreaming or scheming.

"There's only one thing I want for Christmas." Oh, boy. Here we go.

"What's that, buddy?"

"This!" Jared said, pointing to the picture he'd circled in the Target Christmas toy flyer.

"Hmmm...I see. The K'nex Rockin' Roller Coaster. 2,400 pieces. A *hundred-and-ten dollars*?"

"I know it's a lot of money, but you don't have to get me anything else. It's *so* awesome! I really, really want it. Please?" He was practically drooling over the ad. I knew I wouldn't get out of this one easily.

"We'll have to see. I think you should come up with a few more ideas for backups."

"I don't have any more ideas! This is *all* I want! Oh, man . . . it's so cool." He walked away dreaming of his fantastic roller coaster. His single-track focus on this one thing brought to my mind Ralphie from *A Christmas Story,* who wanted a Red Ryder Carbine-Action 200-Shot

Range Model Air Rifle. Like Ralphie's parents, I wasn't sold on the idea. We already had too many little pieces scattered around the house.

I also knew Jared's thrills came in the form of challenges. The fun quickly subsided once he'd achieved the challenge. Would this be another flash-in-the-pan dream come true?

Of course, he persisted, and we got him his K'nex Rockin' Roller Coaster. "Yes! Yes! Yes!" he yelled on Christmas morning as he tore the wrapping paper off of his final "big" gift in two seconds flat. We'd made his day.

Unfortunately, it was, indeed, only a day. He spent the rest of our Christmas afternoon putting together his 2,400-piece contraption, and before we sat down to our Christmas dinner, we all gathered around to watch the roller coaster buzz around the track.

That was the moment he'd envisioned. It was also the moment he lost interest.

Jared was our dreamer; our boy of many passions. When he found an interest, he was all in. From academics to magic to sports, each passion filled every corner of his mind and every hour in his day almost exclusively.

We did our best to encourage him and help him achieve his dreams. We once drove two hours to Chicago to check out a juggling convention. We bought video tapes of ping-pong championships ("Moooommm, it's called *table tennis*"). We drove another three hours to Indianapolis to cheer him on at the National Geographic State GeoBee. In fact, we drove to Indy several times during his stint on a traveling soccer team.

Just like a roller coaster, every new passion brought him higher and higher. And then, once he achieved his goals, he came speeding down, ready to soar up a different hill. But there was one talent that emerged at an early age which he never outgrew.

When Jared was around eighteen months old, I picked him up from the church nursery. The attendant, whose day job was teaching gifted and talented children, grabbed my arm and said, "You've got a mathematician on your hands!"

"What are you talking about?" I asked. Was she referring to my husband Tom, who had been a math major in his early days of college?

"Your son. He built a tower with those nesting cups in no time flat! That's a math skill. He'll be a whiz someday."

I'd seen him build those same nesting cup towers in our toy room at home many times. Blue, green, yellow, red, blue, green, yellow, red, and so on. I was impressed he'd figured them out, but had never equated this play with math skills. "Hmm. I guess we'll wait and see," I said as I kindly thanked my friend.

She called it. When he was around four years old, while visiting Grandpa and Grandma, he walked up to me and said, "Mommy! Did you know three fours is twelve?" I was confused. Who told my son about multiplication? Did he hear it on Sesame Street?

He held up a toy phone with its array of push buttons. Three rows of four. "See Mommy?" He counted to twelve, pressing each button with his tiny fingers.

Since Jared was the first-born, I'm sure the thought that he was a genius crossed our minds a few times during his formative years.

As it turned out, math was not just another one of Jared's fleeting passions. He didn't grow tired of it or give it up. After high school, he studied math at the University of Notre Dame.

In college, he learned the world is a big place and he soon had big dreams of things to see and do. Once he left the safety of home and the watchful eyes of Mom and Dad, his passions and far-fetched ideas had even more room to grow.

For one, he didn't want to get a "real job" right away after graduation. He wanted to walk across America, supported by donations from friends and family. We reminded him he'd have student loans to pay (a *lot* of student loans) and the lenders might not understand why he wasn't looking for a job as he crossed the Appalachian Mountains and worked his way to California. On foot.

We convinced him he needed to find a job, like it or not. So Jared took a job in a math and computer-related industry. We assumed he'd settle down once that first paycheck arrived and all the benefits of a steady job became clear. But it was soon obvious it would take more than a paycheck to deter him from his many passions.

Jared had been working in the corporate world for a couple of years, making a lucrative salary and living in the hip town of Madison, Wisconsin, when he dropped the bomb on us.

"Mom, Dad. I think I'm going to quit my job. I'm going to put out some feelers, but if I don't find a new job by May, I'm going to quit anyway and do some traveling around Southeast Asia for about six weeks."

We were speechless. But he was just beginning to roll.

Sure enough, he was out of Madison by late spring and traveling in Thailand, Japan, Singapore, Malaysia and Indonesia. After a couple of months, he called us from Asia. "I got a job! I'll be working remotely for a company out in Washington State, doing web development. And here's the best part: I've been looking at vans! When I come home, I'm going to buy an old van, trick it out, and live on the road!"

We asked several questions, to which he already had answers.

"I've been researching online. I think I can figure out how to install solar panels on the roof for power, and I can live completely off the grid. It'll be great! No utilities to pay. Just gas in my tank! I can travel all over, visit my friends, hit up some national parks, go climbing. Doesn't that sound awesome?"

Once again, Tom and I had no words.

I look back now and cringe at some of the parenting mistakes I made along the way with Jared. There's a fine line between encouraging your child to be a responsible, sensible adult and squelching all of their dreams and ideas out of the fear they might fail.

When they're younger, we help to cultivate those dreams and passions. We feed into their drive to see everything, do everything, try everything. But little dreamers grow into big dreamers. The risks become greater and the stakes higher.

As Jared grew, so did his passions and their associated risks. Climbing up the face of a cliff is dangerous business. I often pictured my son bloody and broken at the bottom.

Quitting a job is also a risky business. I imagined him unable to find a new job because, who wants to hire someone with multiple short-term jobs on their resume? I've since learned short-term jobs are *not* a deterrent to getting hired in the twenty-first century. I often worried he'd have to move into our basement, destitute and unable to pay back his student loans, and we'd be on the hook for some of those as well. After all, his decision to invest in Bitcoin and other strange currencies instead of a solid retirement plan seemed crazy to us middle-aged savers who made sure our retirement funds were in a balanced portfolio of security and mild risk.

On more than one occasion, whether it was my silence or a disapproving look, he could sense I was not on board with his plans. When he became defensive and angry, I could see the hurt in my dreamer's eyes. "Why can't you ever just believe in me? Why do you think every idea I have is going to be a failure?"

In those moments, I couldn't answer him. To be honest, most of his ventures had been highly successful. And if he failed? Was that so bad?

I thought back to his junior year of high school. Besides math, the other stable interest in his life up to that point had been soccer. He started playing when he was five or six years old and by the time he was in middle school, he'd joined the local travel team.

He spent hours playing in the backyard, sending the ball into the kicking wall Tom had built for him. Anything that was lying on the floor of our home (and with four kids in the house there was plenty), Jared dribbled between his feet, down the hall, and through a doorway, after which we inevitably heard an enthusiastic shout of "*Goooaaalll!*" Soccer meant the world to him.

Until his junior year.

He couldn't wait to make the varsity team; as a dedicated player, he'd put in his time on JV. He thought tryouts had gone well and ran off to practice, excited to be welcomed onto the team.

When he walked in the door that evening, I could see his tear-stained face and red eyes and knew he hadn't made the cut. It was JV again, with little hope of moving up the ranks. My heart broke for him as I heard him sobbing in his bedroom.

How could the coach do this to him? How could anyone hurt a young boy's spirit like this? He'll never want to try out for a sport again. I was sure he'd be crushed for days. Maybe even weeks. Would this scar him for life?

What happened the next day should have taught me something about my boy's resilience.

"Hey, Mom. You know how I kinda wanted to be on the tennis team, but couldn't since it was in the fall like soccer? Well, how about if I just quit soccer and play tennis instead?" His mood was once again bright and spirited in that driven, you-can't-bring-me-down sort of way. The next day, he quit the JV soccer team, joined the tennis team, and didn't look back.

He had tried. He had failed. But he had survived.

The survival skills he learned through the process were more valuable than anything I could have taught him through warnings, fears, and coddling.

In time, this truth finally sank in. To help our kids be the best adults they can be, we have to let them try, watch them succeed, and congratulate them on a job well done. Or let them try, watch them fail, and then help them rediscover their wings so they can fly again.

Jared returned from Asia and moved back in with us. To help him chase his dream, I drove him to Milwaukee so he could buy an old red Chevy Express van. He named it "Blue" and started converting it into his tiny home on wheels.

Our garage turned into a workshop with piles of wood and metal, band saws and jigsaws. He designed handy features like swing-out hanging desks and a bed that converted into a couch. He built contraptions, found what didn't work, took them apart, and started over. I watched in awe at the determination he displayed in making his dreams come true.

After several months, he and Blue were finally ready to roll. He was off to seek adventure, live off-the-grid, visit friends, and work from his tiny home. Once again, he showed us the power of dreams and determination.

Jared and Blue visited twenty-six states, moving from campgrounds to state parks to Walmart parking lots. With a membership at Planet Fitness, he could work out, but more importantly, shower when necessary. He wrote a travel blog, reviewed coffee shops (where he often did his remote work), and found new outdoor wonders to climb and explore.

But his life on wheels wasn't perfect. Internet signals—a necessity for a remote job—were spotty. The solar panels and batteries didn't produce the amount of power he needed. And Blue, faithful though she was, had mechanical issues that added unexpected delays and expenses.

After a solid eight months and nearly 15,000 miles on the road, Jared decided to call it quits. He'd climbed that hill, enjoyed the view, and was ready to take on his next big adventure.

He began looking for a job in any of his few new favorite cities. It didn't take long for him to land another rewarding position, this time in Austin, Texas. He found a house to rent, parked Blue on the street, bought a motorcycle to get around, and settled (at least temporarily as I write this) in the Lone Star State.

Only time will tell what passion will grab hold of him next. To date, he's dabbled in wood-working, photography, app creation, and managing his own Airbnb. He's been in and out of relationships. When "in," he'll become uncertain if she's "the one," and move on. Heartbreak is one of the hardest trials to watch him endure, but I know this young man will one day find someone who will share all of his dreams. It's only a matter of time.

After circling the park on my bicycle, I take off my riding shoes and socks to replace with water shoes. I join my family and together we step cautiously across the stones, marveling at the water beneath our feet. In three months' time, it will travel from the true head of the Mississippi River to the ocean, growing in volume and changing as it goes. Its usefulness through millennia has been surpassed only by its beauty, which has inspired writers and poets, painters and photographers.

I know where this small river will eventually go, and I think of my children. I imagine how they'll grow, where they'll end up, and what they will become. I let go of my fears, knowing that—like Jared—if they slip or fall, they can always get up again.

Take Five! Questions for Reflection

Rivers and Rollers

- What parenting mistakes have you made that make you cringe?

- How have you encouraged your children to go after their dreams? How might you have also squelched those dreams?

- Do you have a child who takes risks that make you uncomfortable? Is it possible you're being overprotective?

- Are you willing to let your child fail? How can failure hurt? How might it bring about growth?

- Has parenting teens and young adults caused any tension or disagreement in your marriage? How have you worked to resolve these issues?

CHAPTER 10

Having All the Right Gear

SETH'S STORY

"Ugh. I'm sick of these sunglasses!" I say as I pluck them from my face and toss them onto the counter.

"What's wrong with them?" Tom asks. He's sitting in my big, comfy chair with his broken arm propped up on a pillow. It's only a few weeks after his accident.

"They only help me see far away. The close-up stuff is blurry," I say as I silently curse getting older. "When I'm riding and get a text or call, I can't just glance at my phone to see if it's worth stopping for. It's a pain!"

"Maybe you should get some progressive *Transitions* like mine."

After his accident, Tom had replaced the scratched-up lenses in his old frames with new light-responsive ones.

"Meh," I say, pulling up my nose. "I've heard they don't block out the UV rays like *real* sunglasses."

"That may be true, but they're good enough for me." It satisfies my practical husband to repurpose his old frames. It's just too bad he won't be able to try them out on rides until the following year.

Being unable to ride in our favorite local organized ride, the Ride for Hospice, a month after his accident, was a bummer for Tom. Their mantra is *Ride. Eat. Repeat* and the "eat" part is fabulous, with local chefs offering healthy treats at the SAG stops.

Tom's inability to ride disappointed me too, as he is my go-to partner, keeping me company and pushing me on to the finish. Having already paid his seventy-five dollar entrance fee, we asked our son Seth if he wanted to ride in Dad's place. He'd inherited Tom's old bike and had been riding a little on his own.

"Sure! Sounds like fun!" It was probably the free beer at the after-party that enticed him, but it didn't matter to me as long as I had someone to chat with on my ride. Besides, Seth and I had faced plenty of challenges together in the past, so I knew we could handle this one, too.

Born on February 14, Seth stole my heart from day one as my little "King of Hearts." As I sat and stared at the perfect little bundle of boy in my arms—so sweet and innocent—I imagined the extraordinary feats he'd accomplish one day.

However, once he became mobile, Tom and I questioned if he'd even survive toddlerhood. We immediately noticed a marked difference between our firstborn and second son. With Jared, we became confident in our above-average parenting skills. Our oldest was a well-behaved child who quietly entertained himself, built patterned towers, and knew his alphabet as a two-year-old. With ignorant pride and foolish arrogance, we privately commented on the less-well-behaved children (and their parents) we encountered.

"Did you hear the Smith's little one screaming in Nursery during church? I could hear her even with the doors closed!" I said, pointing my nose into the air.

"Yeah, and how about that little Billy? He's a wild one. I can't understand why his parents don't do something about him," Tom said, shaking his head.

"Some parents!" I said with an eye roll.

And there we were. The unsympathetic, ill-informed, and inexperienced parents of one well-behaved, angelic child.

Along came child number two.

We swallowed our humble pie and wished we could take back everything we'd said about those other parents, and trade it in for some lessons in raising a child whose middle name was *Mischief.*

Seth had no fear of danger. He'd frequently climb up kitchen drawers, stand on the stove, and reach into cabinets above our range hood to retrieve a favorite snack.

Seth also had no sense of order, regularly throwing all the toys from every shelf and storage container into one enormous pile in the middle of the toy room floor. He sang constantly and loudly, jumping and bouncing and running with more endurance than the Energizer Bunny. His motor never turned off.

I knew by the time he was three that my son had ADHD. I'd read enough books and worked with enough toddlers to see the signs.

"It's a little early to diagnose, as he may outgrow this," our doctor said with nonchalance. "If he's still having trouble when he gets to kindergarten, I'll order testing."

And so we waited. It was a grueling two years.

A child with no impulse control can do a lot of damage and drive the parents crazy. At nap time, Seth would rip the spine from his books, chew the cardboard into a ball, and then stick the ball up his nose. Once or twice he came to me with panic in his tender green eyes, saying, "Mommy, it got stuck!" I'd get out tweezers and cautiously remove the lodged spitball from his nasal passage. If I'd been told this was part of parenting, I may have reconsidered the job!

Although the sound of the vacuum cleaner made Seth run for cover, his tolerance of tactile input—including pain—reached far beyond what I'd consider normal levels. He jumped barefoot from the highest point on our swing set onto the pea gravel below and didn't flinch. He broke his leg when he was two, but sang "God Is So Good" for the whole ER unit to hear as we waited for the x-ray results. He bounced on beds and rollerbladed in our basement (both activities resulting in stitches), all in the name of fun.

Cartoons and Disney sing-along videos mesmerized him, but he could only focus on active play for a minute or two, leaving a trail of mess in his tracks. He chewed on little green army men until they became mangled pieces of plastic. Reprimands, time-outs, and punishments didn't seem to make a difference.

My anger and frustration reached the boiling point many times. In my rage, I'm sure my face turned bright red, my eyes bulged and my neck muscles protruded like pipes ready to burst. I must have resembled a crazy cartoon character because rather than receive the penitent "I'm sorry, Mommy" I needed to hear, Seth would giggle! Afraid I might hurt him if I stayed in his presence, I'd escape to my bedroom, close the door, plop down on my bed, and sob.

When he was four, Seth became a big brother. It stretched me to my limits as I adjusted once again to breastfeeding, diaper changing, and sleepless nights. At the same time, we were building a new house and, having already sold our previous one, were staying at a temporary home. I wanted to enjoy those first glorious moments of being a mom again—to soak in all it meant to have my first daughter. All I wanted was a little peace.

Seth would not give me what I wanted.

During that time, I hit one of my lowest points as a mom. Sitting in the rocking chair nursing my baby girl, I prayed God would help me like my little boy again. I knew I'd always love him; there was no question about that. But there were so many moments I just didn't *like* him. His loudness. His boisterousness. His in-your-face-at-every-moment-ness. It was all more than this too-tired, stressed-out mom could take.

Seth and I loaded our bikes on the car and set off to join the Ride for Hospice. We wanted to get an early start, as the weatherperson was predicting lots of sunshine and 80-degree heat for the afternoon. Tom, arm-in-sling, greeted us from the registration table where he was volunteering. We signed in and picked up maps and the after-party wristbands. Our plan was to ride the shorter twenty-six-mile route, as neither of us had had much time to train since Tom's accident.

But the ride was tougher than we expected. The SAG stops along the way helped, nourishing us with avocado toast, bananas and Nutella, fresh fruit kabobs, and peanut butter cheesecake. We kept our water bottles filled as the sun rose high in the sky and temperatures became unseasonably warm. We were both working as hard as we could, coaxing each other on in this team effort.

"How long 'til the next SAG stop?" Seth asked with a strained look on his sweaty face. Tom's old bike was fine for short rides, but it lacked the gadgets that would make Seth's ride more comfortable. He didn't have a speaker to provide tunes for entertainment and distraction, and the absence of gear bags meant he had to carry a phone and other items in his pockets.

I had the right gear, but struggled with endurance. For me, the hills were grueling enough that, at times, I just wanted to get off the bike and walk. My muscles screamed for me to stop, but I knew better things were waiting if I could just get to the top of the hill and coast for a while. I pictured the finish line and after-party, and pushed myself to continue.

As we rode along, the struggles of Seth's formative years played through my mind. How having the "right stuff" and support was a necessary part of his journey. During those years, I often prayed he'd get the help he needed. And for the help I needed, too.

Shortly after Seth began kindergarten, God answered my prayers. We had him tested, and the results confirmed my suspicions of ADHD. The psychologist looked into the eyes of these two worried parents and gave us the following words: "This diagnosis may seem like a huge deal right now, and you might be concerned about how it'll affect him at school. But keep in mind the big picture. This won't prevent him from doing great things in life."

That future picture was fuzzy, and difficult for me to see or believe.

We started Seth on a low-dose stimulant, and the change was immediately noticeable. In the words of his kindergarten teacher, it was "like night and day!"

Once he could slow down and control his impulses, the sweet little boy I fell in love with at birth stole his way back into my heart. I began to not only love, but also truly *like* this fun-loving, affectionate, and sensitive little boy. God had created him just the way he wanted him to be.

Every morning, Tom and I could count on Seth waking us up by jumping into bed between us. Every night, he stopped by for his goodnight hugs from mom and dad (something he didn't outgrow until he moved to college).

He loved playing video games, collecting Pokémon cards, building Lego sets, and exploring God's creation in our backyard. Like his dad, he was drawn to technology. Like his mom, he had an ear for music and singing, and learned to play my trumpet so he could join the band. Unlike us, he also learned guitar, banjo, mandolin, and ukulele. And boy, did he make us laugh!

He also made us cry. Despite his many abilities, living life with an attention deficit disorder was tough. We'd pray together and have heart-to-heart talks as Seth grappled with the "why me?" of having ADHD. School was a struggle and making friends was difficult, as subtle social cues often flew right past him.

I remember him sitting in the passenger seat as we drove to his counseling session after a particularly rough week. I recall a young boy, wearing the hard shell of a Pokémon Squirtle on the outside, but as soft as a Jigglypuff inside. His eyes filled with tears and his voice cracked as he asked, "Why did I have to get ADHD? Will I have to take medicine for the rest of my life?"

I looked over from the driver's seat at my tender-hearted, sensitive son. "You might, buddy. But that's okay. Your medicine is like glasses. Some kids need glasses to help them see better. You need medicine to help you focus better. The main thing is this: Your ADHD can't stop you from being anything you want to be. You're gonna do great things someday!"

He looked out the window, sniffed, and wiped his eyes, wanting to believe me. As any parent would, I longed to protect my child from the heartache and pain he'd surely encounter in this life, and to give him the tools to manage whatever came his way. As tears welled up in my own eyes, I tried to focus on the road ahead.

Initially, he struggled to write his name, and reading and spelling were also a challenge. But given the right teachers, some tutoring for reading, and lots of tricks for spelling, he eventually caught on. My heart swelled with pride on his graduation day, when he walked the procession as one of the top ten in his high school class.

He moved on to college, where he earned a degree in biology. And two weeks after graduation, he married his college sweetheart, Maddie. It didn't surprise us our "King of Hearts" became the first of our children to find true love and tie the knot.

Seth and I had cleared many hurdles together, but I now faced the new challenge of being a good mother-in-law. Once he and Maddie promised to spend the rest of their lives together, I tried to be a back-seat driver, but Seth quickly put me in my place.

"Mom, I know you think you know what's best for me, but my wife comes first now," he said with an air of confidence that was new to me. "I have to consider her needs, and we need to make our own decisions."

I was a little put off at first. How could anyone come before Seth's mom? After all, he wouldn't be where he was today without me, right? I argued a little and pouted. Then I turned to my own life partner. Tom reminded me we were young once, too. We listened to our parents, but also made our own decisions. Sometimes we messed up. But we survived, and our marriage grew stronger as we worked our way through life together.

As parents of young adults, we learn to let our children go, after equipping them with the gear they need to live as adults. For Seth, his past teachers, tutors, medication, prayers, and heart-to-heart talks helped him on his journey. He had what he needed, and we found the courage to let him find his own way.

The Hospice Ride was an enjoyable mother-son bonding time, as we lugged our out-of-shape bodies up grueling hills together and then coasted down the other side, the wind whistling through our helmets. With a high of 83-degrees in mid-September, the ride's organizers should have changed their mantra to: *Ride. Eat.* **Heat**. *Repeat.* Tired and sweaty, we finally crossed the finish line with a great sense of accomplishment.

Seth had encouraged me along the way, and I'd done the same for him. Though at times we wanted to give up, we knew the after-party was waiting, and so we pushed on. We parked our bikes and forced our wobbly legs to carry us to the food and drink tent where we met up with Tom. After a few bites and sips of that tasty reward, we soon forgot our struggles on the ride.

A year and a half later, in mid-February, Tom and I drove up to Grand Rapids to celebrate Seth's birthday with him and Maddie. It was fourteen degrees outside, but as we pulled into the driveway, Seth came running outside in his jeans and T-shirt to greet us. He was jumping up and down in the snow, bouncing like a three-year-old as he waited for us to get out of the car. I laughed, and said, "He hasn't changed a bit, has he? He's still our bouncy little boy!"

As soon as he got the chance, Seth gave me his usual giant bear hug and said, "Hi, Mom!"

He and Maddie wanted to introduce us to their favorite new neighborhood brewpub, so we headed out for a late lunch and drinks. We chatted about the crazy Michigan weather, the abundance of breweries in their hometown, and the latest happenings in their lives. Seth told us about his hopes for a career that would involve a mixture of biology and technology, and he beamed about their church and his role in the music ministry. The psychologist's words from many years earlier came back to me and I smiled. *Keep in mind the big picture. Someday, he'll do great things.*

Back at their house, he excitedly showed us to his basement, where a brand-new Trek bicycle stood on its training stand. He'd equipped it with all the gadgets he'd asked for at Christmas: bike bag, phone bracket, headlight, taillight, music speaker, and water bottle holder. He'd been working out and preparing for a summer of riding.

On our way home, with the setting sun and mounds of snow creating a blinding brightness, Tom and I both reach for our new sunglasses. I'd gotten mine first and loved them so much, I convinced him to get a pair as well.

They aren't just any sunglasses. We splurged on prescription Ray-Bans with the progressive lenses we'd required since our mid-forties. We love our new shades and agree that our view is much clearer now than before.

With this bit of gear that we'll use on future bike trips, we now have a clear vision of the road ahead. And after our visit with Seth and Maddie, we also enjoy a deeper appreciation of what has always been right in front of us.

TAKE FIVE! QUESTIONS FOR REFLECTION

Having All the Right Gear

- Do you have a child who struggled? Do they still have difficulties as an adult?

- What support and assistance do they need to have in place in order for them to live as independently as possible?

- Do you still worry about your adult child(ren)?

- How can, or should, you continue to support your adult child?

- Is it easier for you to see the big picture now that your child is grown and has flown the nest, compared to when they were younger?

CHAPTER 11

Shelter from the Storm

LEAH'S STORY

I'm twelve miles from home and it's time to head back. As I turn around, I'm surprised to see that the sky has transformed from clear blue to a threatening dark gray. I stop for a quick drink of water and pull up the radar on my phone. It confirms there's a storm brewing.

I had not seen it coming. When I left home, the sun had been shining, the birds were singing, and I saw nothing but a perfect opportunity for a bike ride. I hadn't even checked the forecast as I normally do.

But now, based on the bright bands of green, orange, and red, punctuated by yellow lightning-strike icons, it appears the storm is only fifteen or twenty miles away. I have no idea how fast it's moving, but I know it takes me an hour to bike twelve miles in perfect weather. This is not good.

I've biked through gentle rains, cold, and wind before, but I'm not prepared for a storm. Facing these dark clouds head-on and alone, reminds me of another storm I'd watched my daughter brave mostly on her own. A storm we had not seen coming.

Leah, our third child and first daughter, charmed us from day one. As a baby, she smiled at everyone who glanced her way. As a toddler, she was quiet and cautious. One day, as she was learning to walk, she lightly bumped her head on the coffee table and cried for a bit, as expected. But what surprised me was that she hesitated to cruise around the coffee table for the next several days.

Wow! She's so different from her brother. Seth would have jumped right back up again! I was relieved to know she didn't have ADHD.

She loved to bang on the piano and make up songs, so at age five, after she begged, without relenting, for piano lessons, I gave in and started teaching her myself. I quickly discovered the intensity of her interest was real. By the time she was in first grade, we were taking Leah to lessons, along with her two older brothers. Playing the piano made her happy.

But the second-grade teacher saw another side of our happy, budding musician.

"I'm concerned about Leah," she said at our parent-teacher conference. She glanced at us before looking down at her papers. Biting her lip, she said, "Leah can be very moody. She often goes into the corner and sulks. To be honest, I've not seen this in a child before, and I don't know what to make of it."

Leah was capable academically, but would often shut down when she had work to do. Since we'd seen similar behaviors at home, including frequent meltdowns, I began my quest to "fix" her. I started with an Internet search on "moody little girls who shut down when they're overwhelmed." Much to my surprise, Leah's behaviors lined up perfectly with "girls with ADHD."

How could that be? She was nothing like her brother. I kept searching and learned ADHD can look vastly different from one child to another. We scheduled an evaluation, and the results confirmed our new suspicions. Leah was having trouble staying focused, causing her to become overwhelmed. This, in turn, brought on anxiety that made her retreat to the corner of her classroom and sulk. We had an answer, and though it was the last thing any of us expected or desired, I was glad now to know how to help her.

With some medications to help with focus, her mood improved, and Leah had survived this first "whammy." But like a small rain shower that precedes a big storm, there was more to come.

Seventh grade rolled around. Leah had just switched schools and was now attending our local public school, where they routinely completed scoliosis screenings each spring. One day, after school, she handed me a note from the nurse that said:

Your child: _**LEAH**_

__ **Passed the scoliosis screening.**

X Did not pass the scoliosis screening.

This is only a screening.

**We recommend you follow up with a visit to your doctor.**

I thought little of it. Seth had also failed his screening, but after a visit to the orthopedic doctor, we were told he was fine. I assumed the same was true of Leah, so I didn't rush to schedule an appointment.

A typical shopping trip to Target, however, was enough to wake me up. The summer was fast approaching, and the girls needed new bathing suits. I peeked into the dressing room and saw Leah from behind with a scant bit of clothing on. I did a double take. *What's wrong with her right hip? Why does it jut out so much farther than her left?*

"Stand up straight," I said.

"I am."

"Are you sure?"

"Yes, Mom," she responded with the obligatory preteen eye-roll.

"We need to make you a doctor's appointment."

And thus began the journey into Leah's "double-whammy."

After countless orthopedic visits, x-rays, and two back braces worn nearly 24/7 for two years, we were hoping to hear, "All is good! Your spine is straight and should stay that way!" Instead, we were told the braces had not worked. Another year of doctor appointments and x-rays confirmed Leah's center of gravity was off, and she was going to continue to lean and tilt unless the pediatric orthopedic surgeon could stabilize her spine through surgery.

We scheduled her spinal-fusion surgery for mid-summer, before her junior year of high school. She would have two fifteen-inch rods fused to her spine with thirty-two screws. She'd spend six days at Peyton Manning's Children's Hospital in Indianapolis. The doctor assured us she'd feel great and be able to go back to school in September, eight weeks after her surgery.

What none of us knew was that we would soon contend with the third part of what became Leah's "triple whammy."

The sky is getting darker and more ominous by the minute, and the wind is picking up. I check the radar again. There's no way I'll make it home before the rain hits. I need to find shelter and I need to find it soon.

My goal is to reach a restaurant that I know has a covered patio. I'm about two miles away from it, and based on my best calculations, I might make it there before the rain falls. Calling on a reserve of strength in my legs to get me there, I say a brief prayer. After all, it was prayers—ours and those of our friends and family—that brought us through Leah's most challenging storm.

Her spinal-fusion surgery went well, but the recovery was difficult. I lived by her side in the hospital room for the six days of her stay. She was often thirsty, so I brought her fresh water, and the nurses and I kept her as comfortable as was possible for a girl with an eighteen-inch incision down her back. I couldn't wait for her release, but she was so uncomfortable, she didn't seem to care when we would return home. Her bright and cheerful smile had completely disappeared, and I tried everything to get it back.

"Hey Leah, do you want to go down to the kids' room? They've got puzzles!" No response.

"How 'bout I turn on some of your favorite songs to help you relax?"

"I don't care," she said with a groan.

"It's activity time. Would you like to go make some crafts?"

"No. I just want to stay in bed." Clenching the sheets in her fists, she turned her face away from me.

Nothing brightened her countenance. Her face had cemented into an immovable frown. It broke this mother's heart.

Release day finally came. Her greatest wish? To stop for a Coke and some Little Debbie's snack cakes. I obliged. I'd happily break all the healthy parenting rules to find my girl's smile again. There was a glimmer of a smile when I replied, "Anything you want, dear!"

We expected continued recovery once she was home in her own bed, but her progress came to a standstill. Her incision was not healing, she had no energy, and she felt beyond miserable. Despite her voracious appetite, the numbers on the scale decreased daily. Her surgeon and his assistants had told us it was normal for a patient to lose ten pounds during the initial recovery period, but that she'd regain it soon afterward. She didn't. Instead, she lost even more weight.

She'd grown at least an inch from the straightening of her spine, her height now measuring five-foot-nine, but her weight had plummeted to eighty-nine pounds. She looked anorexic. Friends and family often asked if she was eating; I assured them she was.

After her first two grueling weeks back at school, I couldn't watch her suffer any longer. My mother's intuition told me something was terribly wrong, even if I couldn't put a finger on it. I made an appointment with our family doctor and poured out all our concerns. I asked if he could order some blood tests, thinking she might have a vitamin, potassium, or iron deficiency. He agreed, took the blood samples, and said he'd call if they found anything.

That evening, as Leah and I sat at home instead of attending the high school football game with the rest of the family, I received the phone call that changed her life.

"Is this Leah's mother?" a man's voice on the other end asked.

"Yes."

"I'm the doctor on call this evening. We have the results of Leah's blood work here, and a couple of the numbers show your daughter might have diabetes. You need to bring her to the emergency room as soon as possible."

I was sure there had been some miscommunication.

"Umm, you know she just had major spinal fusion surgery, right? She's been having problems recovering. It's all just related to that. There's no history of diabetes with her or anyone in our family."

"Yes, I'm aware she just had surgery. But these numbers from her blood work show she may have diabetes. She needs to be checked out as soon as possible."

I was pretty sure the doctor didn't understand our situation and didn't know what he was talking about. My baby had already been through so much. How could this be true as well?

I called Tom, who was sitting in the stadium next to our neighbor, Bob, who is also a doctor. I told Tom I was taking Leah to the emergency room, but didn't think it was necessary for him to come along. It was probably just a false alarm, and not worth missing the game.

Tom mentioned it to Bob. After hearing "a couple of numbers point to diabetes," Bob immediately understood that one number was likely her blood glucose level. The other indicated ketoacidosis—a life-threatening condition that occurs when blood sugar is out of control. He didn't explain all this to Tom, but in his wise and thoughtful manner, said, "I think you should meet them at the ER. You should be there."

Tom left the game and met us at the hospital. The medical staff tested Leah's blood glucose level again and found it to be 711 (the normal range is around 70-120). They then gave us the life-changing news: Leah had type 1 diabetes.

That night, we entered the eye of the storm.

I looked at my gaunt and sickly daughter from across the room in the ER. How long had this been going on? And how could we have not known? It was all adding up. The thirst in the hospital was unquenchable, as I refilled her large water cups over and over. She ate and ate and ate after returning home, but kept losing weight. Her incision was not healing.

As we came to understand how diabetes works, we learned her body was no longer producing insulin—the chemical needed to turn her food and sugar into energy—and instead was burning her fat and muscle for energy. That explained the twenty pounds she'd lost since her surgery. The high blood sugars had made her sick and lethargic to an extreme, and her body couldn't heal when it was using every reserve to stay alive.

In retrospect, there had been signs of prediabetes before the surgery. The doctors explained she'd been, in essence, standing on the edge of a cliff before surgery. The procedure caused enough trauma to her body that it pushed her over that precarious edge.

Leah looked at me from across the small, sterile hospital room, tears welling in her eyes. "So, does this mean I can't eat donuts and stuff anymore?" Life couldn't get much worse for my sweet-tooth daughter who, on top of everything else, now feared a life without donuts.

The nurses and dietician assured her that while she couldn't have donuts in the hospital, she could eventually eat anything she wanted. They gave her insulin and moved her to a hospital room. Over the next couple of days, she started gaining weight, and her stamina and strength returned as well.

For the first time in ten weeks, I saw my girl's beautiful smile again.

She took ownership of the disease from day one and quickly learned all the ins and outs of blood sugar checks, insulin dosing, and injections. This disease, for which there is no cure, would require her daily, even hourly, attention. After a few months, she received an insulin pump, which she learned to program and maintain. She found support groups online, met new friends (her "diabuddies"), and celebrated mini victories along the way.

With her diabetes under control, Leah was back in school and thrived; she completed her junior and senior years with a straightened spine and the occasional donut. She danced and sang in high school musicals, played flute in the concert band, and mallet instruments in the marching band pit. She became more serious about piano as she auditioned for college music programs.

Her big move to college required extra effort and planning to ensure safety nets were in place to control her blood sugar. It also meant finding an extra-large storage organizer for all of her pump and insulin supplies.

Although the initial storm had passed, it often seemed the rains followed her. Due in part to her ADHD, she endured college struggles, changed majors, and switched schools. Added to her stress was the death of one of her high-school best friends in a tragic car accident. As her mother, it was hard watching my beloved child drowning in grief, anxiety, sadness, and stress. Many times I tried to rescue her. But my help could only get her so far.

Still, Leah had endearing qualities that brought joy whenever she was around. Her visits home filled our house with piano music and singing. She spent hours making jigsaw puzzles on the basement table. When she wasn't memorizing lines from every Disney movie we owned, she was making her own movies by transferring bits of our home videos into her own creations: HFHV (Hanstra's Funniest Home Videos). The girl who once couldn't smile made us laugh until we cried.

It took some time, but the storm that had overtaken us finally cleared, and the sun peeked through the clouds again. Through all these experiences, Leah learned that her only true source of strength and comfort was her faith, which grew stronger. She saw a purpose in the difficulties she'd endured, believing God had been preparing her to help shine his light through the storms others might be facing.

In sharing her story, she told of the impact God had on her life. She spent two summers at a local camp helping underprivileged youth come to know Jesus and listened as they shared their own life difficulties.

She finally settled on her college major: music therapy. The calling to this field was in part because of her own experience with trials and suffering, but also because of the healing she herself experienced through music, her first love.

I'm riding as fast as I can. Wet spots are forming on the road and an occasional raindrop hits my arms and shoulders. Thankfully, I can see the restaurant just ahead on the left.

I safely cross the road, dismount from my bike, and quickly step under the canopy of the patio just as the clouds let loose. An occasional wind gust blows raindrops my way, but I'm protected by the surrounding shelter.

My mind wanders and I recall the voice of the doctor on the phone that night: "We have the results of Leah's blood work. You need to bring her to the emergency room as soon as possible." The memory still rocks me. It was the storm we didn't see coming.

Our family, friends, and church gave us shelter as they poured out their love and prayers for Leah. And through faith, she found her life's calling and a purpose to all the pain and suffering.

As parents, Tom and I tried to treat each of our children with equal shares of love and gifts, and we believed it was our job to fix the things that were broken. So it was hard to answer Leah's tough questions.

A few weeks after her diabetes diagnosis, she sat on the couch across from me with tears welling up in her eyes. "Why me? Why did everything have to happen to me? Why couldn't one of the other kids have one of these problems? It's not fair."

I didn't have an answer to any of those questions. And the problems she faced, I couldn't fix. The fact is, life isn't always fair. There's no explanation for why one person suffers while another one doesn't. There are storms that come and go and there are showers that remain. Some storms turn into devastating floods and not every ending brings sunshine and rainbows.

In time, Leah came to terms with her "storm" when she found her Shelter. Even the clouds in her life made sense when she saw glimpses of the Light streaming through them. As her parents, we learned that when there's something we can't fix, we can hand our child over to our loving Father. Through our own prayers, individually and as a couple, and by asking our family and friends to pray, we slowly learned to put doubts aside as we placed our children in God's hands.

I sit under the canopy and watch the storm pass, knowing eventually the worst will be over and I'll soon be able to get back on the road. I give thanks to God. His sheltering love and protection have helped us courageously navigate every sprinkle, cloudburst, and storm.

TAKE FIVE! QUESTIONS FOR REFLECTION

Shelter from the Storm

- Have you endured "storms" such as unexpected injuries, illnesses, or loss during your parenting journey?

- How did you find shelter for your child during the storm? For yourself? Who or what are the shelters you look for in the face of storms?

- If your child/family has come through an unexpected difficulty, can you see ways in which you or your child grew through the experience?

- Does your adult child still have scars that need healing? How can you encourage them to get the help they need?

- If you're familiar with the Bible, can you think of a character whose story is one of storms and trials? What verses come to mind reminding you of God's care and provision during life's difficulties?

CHAPTER 12

Fears and What-ifs

CHLOE'S STORY

We've arrived in Minnesota for our annual vacation, joined as usual by some of our extended family. Tom had taken a long solo ride earlier in the day, so I asked my sister and brother-in-law to join me on a short ride to try out a new trail. As we leave the resort, I clip the cleat of my right shoe onto the bracket of the pedal and push off. After a couple of rotations, my left foot finds its bracket and—snap!—I'm clipped in and rolling.

I exchanged my old pedals with clipless pedals over a year ago. Confused by their name at first, I soon learned that "clipless pedals" *aren't* pedals without clips. Rather, they're pedals unlike their predecessors—the ones with a big toe clip and strap that goes over the shoe. Clipless pedals require the rider to clip a cleated shoe in and out. So, even though the shoes and pedals *clip* together, manufacturers named them *"clipless"* to differentiate them from the old-style toe clips.

I ultimately get past the confusing name, and even clipping in and clipping out has become second nature to me. No more searching with the ball of my foot for the precise placement of my cleat against the clip. The new pedals are great for gaining speed and climbing hills. I use not only the downward motion to push the pedals toward the ground, but I also bring them up as my feet—attached to the pedals through my shoes—pull upward.

Riding with the clipless pedals is a skill that makes me feel I've arrived! Reaching this high note on my cycling journey reminds me of another type of high note that began with a text message from my youngest child, one late November day.

My phone had buzzed, alerting me to a text from Chloe to our "FamBam" group—the text group that included my husband and me, as well as our four kids and daughter-in-law.

> *Hey Fam!!! If you want to watch me sing really high notes while wearing a potato sack, tune in on Sunday at 3:00 p.m. We're singing some amazing songs this year and if you wonder what part I'm singing, just listen for the high notes ;) Hope you can watch!!*

Attached was a selfie. Our daughter Chloe's wavy red hair contrasted with the cream-colored choir robe, reminiscent of a monk's robe or, you might say, "a potato sack." Draped over her shoulders was a royal blue stole, cinched with a rope around her waist.

I could sense her excitement, which was in perfect harmony with mine. Tom and I would be there to witness her second Christmas Festival at St. Olaf College in person, and I was already anticipating the thrill of the experience. Having attended her first festival the previous year, as well as the one before that when she was a prospective student (aka a "prospie"), I knew what a treat it was going to be. This was a concert unlike any we'd experienced during our kids' growing-up years. And we'd experienced many.

Our kids' programs started with preschool, Sunday school, and elementary school. Then we worked our way through dance and piano recitals before rounding off our time with high school band and choir concerts, marching band competitions, and best of all, high school musicals.

Blessed with a keen musical ear and powerful voice, Chloe was, to my dismay, not blessed with the desire to perform. At least not in public. At home, she was all drama—putting on shows for our family, hamming it up, and standing on her chair at the dinner table whenever she demanded our attention. And being the youngest of four children, she demanded it often.

But on stage, in the public eye, all her defenses went up. I could see the musical and theatrical potential, but, try as I might, I could not get her into the spotlight. Whether afraid of failure or embarrassment, she'd stare at her toes and scarcely move her mouth as Tom, armed with our 8mm video camera, panned over the group of miniature-sized shepherds, angels, and wise men during the Sunday school Christmas programs.

Seeing her flair for music, we gave dance lessons a try. We soon discovered dance was also not her thing, as she cowered in the doorway of the dance studio, resistant to every type of coercion and coaxing a dance teacher and I could employ. Even with big sister Leah at her side, she was just too self-conscious to let anyone besides family see her dance.

Then there were piano lessons, and the struggle intensified. One day, we pulled up to the piano teacher's house and Leah hopped out of the car with her bag of music books, eager to take the first lesson. Chloe and I remained in the car. She'd practiced little that week and knew she would not play her songs perfectly. Perfection was the standard by which she measured talent and abilities, and if she couldn't achieve it, then the activity wasn't worth doing. This usually resulted in an all-out war with the one person who wanted to see those musical talents develop more than anyone else—me.

"I can't do it!" she yelled. "I *hate* piano! I'm *not* going in there! I hate it, I hate it, I *hate* it!"

I looked at her red, tear-stained face in the rearview mirror. She expressed several other self-abasing comments that tore at my heart and made me question everything I'd ever done in the name of encouraging my child to use her gifts. As I had many times before, I talked her down (and probably threw in a bribe), until I could get her into the house and seated at the piano, where she muddled through an imperfect lesson.

I should have expected the struggle. As a toddler, Chloe was my most sensitive child. Her sensory issues made her scream "Ouchy toes!" when she could feel the seams in her socks and she threw temper tantrums if I tried to put a pair of jeans on her. She also feared being alone, so whenever she needed to be upstairs or get something from the basement, someone had to go with her. We learned to adapt to her quirky fears and sensitivities, but anxiety and avoidance followed her into every new situation. Even if that new situation involved something she loved, like music.

As I recalled her fears, I reflected on my own.

"Clipless pedals are great!" my cousin had said as we compared his bike gear to mine. "You just have to be okay with knowing you're going to fall at least once."

"But I hate falling! I don't know if I can be *okay* with that." I mulled it over and put it off for a while.

Then Tom and I joined a small organized ride near my hometown. It was a beautiful day, and I was pedaling hard to keep up with him. I averaged a little over 13 miles per hour on the 64-mile ride—an excellent speed for me. But since Tom typically rode about 15 miles per hour, I knew I was slowing him down.

We finally finished the ride in a little over six hours, including some resting time. "I just wish I could go faster so these rides wouldn't take us so long," I said to the gals at the checkout table.

"Do you have clipless pedals?" one of them asked.

"No. I'm afraid of falling," I replied.

"Oh, well, there is that. But you get used to them and then you don't fall so much. They increased my speed by about two miles an hour. I'll never go back!"

I was envious, but just wasn't sure I could sign myself up for falling. I mean, who in their right mind does something intentionally that will probably cause them harm?

Ultimately, the hills changed my mind. My knees hurt from the stress I put on them as I pushed and pushed to get to the top. I longed for an easier way to climb, and I decided a fresh approach might be worth a try.

For Christmas that year, I told the family I wanted clipless pedals and biking shoes. When the goods arrived, Tom installed the pedals on my bike, which was on the trainer in the basement. As I rode on the trainer throughout the winter, I noticed a change. My legs felt more secure. Strength built up not only in my quads as I pushed down but also in my hamstrings, as I pulled my pedals up. I became better at clipping in and clipping out. Having success on the trainer provided me with the confidence I needed to branch out and try this new thing I'd been afraid of for so long.

The true test came when spring arrived. I couldn't wait to get outside and on the road again. With trepidation, I mounted my bike and placed my right foot into the pedal clip. I pushed down and my bike began to roll. Lifting myself up onto the seat, I brought my left foot up. After several attempts to connect my cleat with the clip, it finally clicked. Next, to clip out. As I slowly cruised along our private country road, I turned my left heel outward and felt my shoe unclip.

I practiced several times up and down our short half-mile road. Clip in right. Clip in left. Clip out left. Clip out right. I was doing it! And the best part? I wasn't falling!

But the thing about clips is you don't know when something unexpected is going to interrupt your smooth routine of clipping in and clipping out. My first fall was a silly little mishap when I failed to coordinate the clipping out with my stopping and standing. I gently plopped down on the soft grass beside the trail we were on. Tom was the only one who saw me fall, so there was little harm to my body or my pride.

The second time, I was biking by myself and came to a stop sign just as a large 4x4 pickup pulled up beside me. Again, I gently, but ungracefully, plopped onto the grass.

"Are you okay?" the passenger inquired through his open window.

"I'm fine! Thanks!" The fall didn't hurt me physically, but embarrassment hung over me for the rest of the ride.

Slowly, I gained confidence, my strength improved, and my average speed increased. I still wasn't going 15 miles per hour, but I no longer had to worry about my feet slipping off my pedals when going fast, standing up to stretch, or biking in wet conditions.

My jitters gradually faded, just as my daughter's dread of performing diminished with time and experience.

In the fifth grade, Chloe joined the band and started as a percussionist. She was hiding in the back row, but she was there. She kept it up throughout her middle and high school days, even during marching season when she was front and center with the pit. She loved it. Playing in the band boosted her confidence, and she surprised us all when she took up piano again to play with the jazz band during her senior year.

But her true passion? It all came back to singing. Sometime around seventh grade, she found her voice. She and her "BNF" (Best Neighbor Forever—a term they'd coined for each other) were selected to sing a duet at the spring choir concert. The two girls spent many after-school hours sitting at our piano, practicing their harmony and memorizing the words to "Mighty to Save,"[1] a worship song they'd chosen for their debut. We took a Saturday trip to the mall to buy coordinating outfits and after much debate, they chose a black-and-neon-yellow combo, a trendy fashion statement at the time.

They were ready when the big night arrived and pulled it off beautifully. Thus began a new chapter in Chloe's life as a performer, one that often included her BNF at her side. With the support of someone she trusted alongside her, she gradually put her fears aside and instead leaned into the joy of music she'd been born to share.

In their senior year, they sang together as two of the three older sisters in *Fiddler on the Roof.* Chloe's dramatic bent as a child finally found its way to the "big" stage, and although she was still more reserved in public than at home, she enjoyed that shining moment on the stage.

As the mom who had encouraged—maybe even pushed—her for years, I was bursting with pride as she sang her way through "Matchmaker, Matchmaker,"[2] and felt a lump in my throat during "**Sabbath Prayer**."[3] I held back the tears through "**Sunrise, Sunset**,"[4] as I realized how quickly the years were flying by. Then, much to my surprise, my daughter floated seamlessly through "Chava's Dance," a spotlight sequence featuring none other than the little girl who had refused to enter the dance studio years earlier.

We waited with great anticipation for the choirs of St. Olaf College to file in for their first of four nights of sold-out performances. As they did, I soon found my baby girl amongst the other cream-colored "potato sacks" and snapped a quick photo. The orchestra began, followed by five choirs: Manitou, in green robes; The Viking Chorus, in blue; Chapel Choir, in cranberry; the St. Olaf Choir, in royal purple; and Cantorei, wearing off-white "potato sacks" with blue stoles—over 500 performers in all. For the next two hours, the words and music mesmerized and lifted me to a sacred moment about as close to heaven as I could imagine.

Now one among many in a mass choir, Chloe's smile revealed a glow of pure joy. I could tell any nervousness was only because of her excitement in knowing we were out in the crowd. Those days when she looked down at her toes were long gone, and I was thankful for the young woman she'd become. Looking at ease, she swayed in time with the tempo and communicated her love and appreciation for the music through eyes gleaming with gratefulness.

Whether alone in the spotlight, or as one of 500—wearing a potato sack, no less—she'd found her voice. Her joy. Her gift.

Getting there had not been easy. But few rewarding journeys are.

As we ride, my sister, brother-in-law, and I discover the newly paved Minnesota bike trail is as smooth as a piano's ebony keys, and the afternoon breeze carries the lake air like a song. After about two miles, the new trail ends and we turn the corner.

The older trail isn't as smooth as the new one, but it enables us to stay off the road and away from cars. Around the four-mile point, just before an intersection, I look up and see a hefty black dog standing watch with his owner on the back steps of a house. When the unleashed dog spots us, it immediately runs toward us with a menacing bark.

As we speed up to escape the vicious-looking beast, I see a six-inch curb before us at the intersection instead of the typical ramp for trail riders. I yell "Curb!" and, unable to stop or go around it, all three of us fly over the curb and safely land upright with a *thud! Thud! Thud!*

If the dog and the first curb weren't scary enough, we next have to navigate the curb going *up* to the bike path on the other side of the road. I know going up a curb of that size is downright dangerous, if not impossible, so I yell, "Curb! Stopping!" On impulse, I turn to avoid the curb and slam on my brakes. Unable to unclip my shoe from my pedal fast enough, I teeter for a split second before tipping over. With no free foot to stop my fall, my left leg, arm, and handlebar hit the pavement.

My sister, who has somehow successfully jumped the curb, and my brother-in-law, who stops on the road near me, help me up. My Apple Watch senses my fall and starts buzzing *SOS*. I hit the "I'm okay" response.

Each time I fall, whether it's a minor plop or a major crash, I'm shaken, and fear creeps in. I imagine all the "what ifs": *What if I'd been more severely injured? What if the dog had attacked me as I lay there on the ground? What if next time no one else is around to help me? What if I'm not able to hit the "I'm okay" response on my watch?*

It's not possible to embark on new adventures without some risk. When I mount my bike, I pray for safety. For protection from falls, cars, and vicious animals. Just as I pray through my anxieties in other life adventures—in writing, traveling, retiring, parenting my adult children, and empty nesting.

Chloe's experience with new endeavors is like mine, and she's also learned prayer is a great defense against fear. While she's conquered her fears of performing on stage, anxiety creeps in again with every new undertaking: "What if I don't get into my first choice of college?" "What if I don't get along with my roommate?" "What if I don't find a job?" "What if I can't afford the graduate school I want to attend?"

In answer to our prayers, God provides for and protects us. He promises not a hair will fall from our heads (nor a knee will smash into pavement), without his knowing. He gives us the encouragement we crave and the companionship we desire. In fact, he supplies our every need.

Indeed, our God enables us to receive encouragement, or the gentle push, we need from those who love us. They have our best interests in mind, so their confidence in us spills over into our own self-confidence. We also need companions, like Chloe's BNF. For me, it's my husband, family, friends, and writing communities. Our fears subside when we have others who can pick us up when we fall or carry the burdens weighing us down.

With that confidence—though I'm skinned up and bruised—I get back on my bike, and once again clip right, push off, clip left, and say a prayer. Slowly, the three of us make our way back to the resort where I cover my scrapes with ointment and bandages.

I remind myself that a ride without risk is rare. Our journeys, though riddled with mistakes, imperfections, and ill-timed moves, offer opportunities to trust more in ourselves, our closest allies, and our Heavenly Father.

Knowing this, we can push through our worries and fears, and our "what ifs" begin to sound a little different: *What if we learn something new? What if life turns out better than we expect? What if our dreams come true?*

When we reach for the high notes, we just might hit them. And the rewards might be better than we imagined.

TAKE FIVE! QUESTIONS FOR REFLECTION

Fears and What-ifs

- We've all had humbling moments as parents. What is one that stands out to you?

- Can you think of a time your encouragement helped your child overcome a fear or build confidence?

- Can you recall a time your pushing may have hurt your child's confidence?

- What fears or anxieties have you had to overcome and what supports were most helpful to you?

- How can you see God working through your fears or those of your child?

CHAPTER 13

Against the Wind

RETURN OF THE FLEDGLING

There's an old Irish blessing that says, "May the road rise to meet you. May the wind be always at your back." Today, I can hear the wind whistling through the trees, but it doesn't sound like a gentle invitation. Instead, it sounds more like a warning that today might not be the best day for a ride.

So what do I do? I ignore the warnings.

The temperature is perfect. The sun is shining. I have nothing pressing on my agenda and I need the exercise. I'm going for a ride. Wind or no wind.

I want to go about ten miles, so I take my usual route, heading east with the wind at my back. It feels great to soar. Ha! What wind?

Oh. *That* wind.

As soon as I turn back, I realize my folly.

The helpful tailwind is now a menacing headwind. I can hardly pedal against it. It reminds me of one of the hard lessons Tom and I learned as parents of young adults.

When the boys came home from college that first summer, we discovered college kids no longer find it necessary to tell parents where they're going or what time they'll be home. When they're away at school, we don't know their every move—what time they get back to their dorms and when they crawl into their beds. But when they're under our roofs and watchful eyes, we want to know. A mother can lie awake for hours if she knows (or thinks) her babies should be home.

After a few arguments, I adjusted the rules and expectations. The kids learned the common courtesy of letting us know where they were going and when they might return. And we learned we didn't need to know specifics, which they considered prying into their business.

Each summer, we also noticed a sudden increase in the quantities of food, dirty dishes, and loads of laundry. Our "boomerang" kids—as they're called—largely ignored our rules about picking up after themselves.

The next go-around, when Leah moved home for the summer, my expectations were realistic. I knew what was coming. I was prepared to give her space and got ready to increase my workload. It would be worth it to spend time with my daughter again. Time to chat and get to know this new adult person she was becoming. Since she's the only serious piano player in the family, I also imagined her gracing us with serenades after dinner.

I was ready and looking forward to a great summer with no problems. Ha! What problems?

Oh. *Those* problems.

First, there was her bedroom. I had naively assumed if I thoroughly cleaned and organized it while she was at school, she'd return and love it so much she'd never let it get messy again. I organized her desk, the closet, and even some dresser drawers. I dusted blinds and vacuumed cobwebs. I made the bed with hospital corners and arranged twelve throw pillows with meticulous attention to symmetry. This room could compete with the best Airbnb's I'd seen online.

After two weeks, it was all undone. And so was I, when I finally opened the door to her room, which she'd wisely kept closed.

I stood aghast at the sight. The floor was strewn with clothing (clean and dirty), books, spiral binders, pop cans, trash, crocheting, and twelve throw pillows. Blankets and sheets lay in a rumpled mess over the bed, tangled in computer and phone cords. The only remaining proof of my hard work was the dust-free blinds and corners without cobwebs, since not enough time had passed for the dust to settle again.

Thus began my summer of nagging.

"Clean your room!"

"Shouldn't you be practicing your piano?"

"Put the food away."

"Don't you have some work you can do?"

"You're watching a movie again?"

In turn, it became her summer of passive resistance.

"I *am* cleaning my room!" (Said for the third day in a row.)

"I already practiced." (For about fifteen minutes.)

"I wasn't the last one to eat."

"No, I have plenty of time to prepare for next year."

"It's summer break!"

I'm not sure who was more relieved at summer's end—Leah or myself. After a year apart, we discovered we'd both become set in our new ways. The constant resistance of my will against hers was like pedaling against the wind.

Feeling like I've been going uphill without ever reaching the top, I downshift so my pedals will spin slightly easier. I'm making very little progress and irritated that it's not the fun ride I imagined it would be.

As I approach the downhill slope that I often coast on, I'm ready for some relief. But this headwind is so strong, it won't even let me coast. Even in the lowest gear, going downhill, I still have to pedal to keep moving. *This* is resistance. I make a mental note to choose my rides more wisely next time.

I realize I should have invited Tom to join me. When two or more bikers face a strong headwind together, they can take turns "drafting" for each other. The lead biker breaks through the wind, while the next one follows close behind, thus facing less resistance. Tom has often drafted for me, and I wish I had him along on this ride.

The next two summers were easier. Since Leah found a job at a local summer camp, she only came to visit us on weekends. It was the best of both worlds. We got to see each other, but her room remained relatively clean. We didn't get on each other's nerves and learned to appreciate our time together.

Then came the fourth summer. With the many storms in her life—ADHD, scoliosis, diabetes, the death of her friend, and the accompanying stress—she had not yet finished school and instead signed up for the "extended college plan." With another year and a half of college to go, she needed more money than she could make as a camp counselor. She'd live at home again, all summer.

By then, Chloe had gone off to college and wouldn't be coming home for the summer. The boys were adulting and living on their own. It would be just the three of us: Leah, Tom, and me. I was determined to make it work. There had to be a way the three of us could live together without constantly butting heads.

I knew my "little girl" was moving toward adulthood and wanted to be in control of her life. My goals for Leah were similar; I wanted her to be an independent, thinking adult. I decided there would be no more Mom-making-the-rules-and-telling-her-what-to-do. I came up with a plan and asked Tom if he thought it would help.

"You can try it. And I'll back you up if things get rough again."

After she unloaded her car, I asked Leah to sit and chat with me. I was in my comfy chair. She lounged on the couch, petting the cat.

"So, if we're all going to make things work this summer, we need to have a plan. I know what I need from you. But I want to know what you need from me." I was ready, with a notepad and pen in hand.

She continued to pet the cat, silently gathering her thoughts.

"I don't want you to ask me about my piano," she said after a few minutes. "I'm fully aware my junior recital is in the fall, and I've worked out a plan with my teacher. I know what I have to do to prepare." She stopped and glanced at me to check my reaction. When she saw me nodding my head, she continued.

"I don't want you to ask me about my classes." *Okay.* I could leave that alone.

"I want alone time in my room." No surprise there. My introverted daughter frequently needed this.

"And I want you to make me spaghetti for dinner," she said with a little grin. I smiled too. That, I could manage.

Then I laid out my needs. "I expect you to do your own laundry, put dishes away, and put your food away.

"And although I don't expect you to make dinner, I'd love it if you'd offer to help now and then out of the goodness of your heart. Ask if you can help set the table, make a salad to go with the meal—stuff like that. Act like you would if you were a guest in someone's house, because, well, that's what you are."

She nodded, and short of signing a contract and shaking hands, we'd come to an agreement.

Our summer passed smoothly. It wasn't perfect, but I could usually see the carpet on her bedroom floor. She practiced her piano music without prompting or nagging. And I made her spaghetti.

She worked hard that summer, babysitting thirty or more hours a week, playing piano, and reading ahead for her fall classes. While Tom and I were on our annual two-week vacation, she guarded the house, mowed the grass, and cared for the pets. She was learning to adult, and that made a smoother ride for all of us.

Besides her daytime jobs and activities, Leah also filled out her evenings. After auditioning for the local community theater's production of the musical *Oliver!* and landing the supporting role of "Bet," she was busy with rehearsals and performances.

As the summer wound down and I watched her on that stage—hair perfectly curled and wearing a smile as bright as her satin dress—I relished in how far we'd come. Singing "It's a Fine Life,"[1] she reminded me of the little girl who loved to bang on the piano and sing her heart out.

Over the years, we had guided. She had strayed. We'd pushed in one direction while she pulled in the other. Like the wind in my face, we'd resisted each other's best intentions and slowed each other down. But once we figured out that we both wanted the same outcome—for her to become an independent adult leading a fulfilling life—the weight lifted and we encouraged each other down the path we were on.

I finally make it home, exhausted but wiser. I now know to check wind speeds before I ride and to stay home if they're over 12–13 miles per hour. I also plan my rides according to the direction of the wind, riding against the wind first, when I'm energized and strong. Then, when I get tired, I can ride with the wind at my back, which will push me home. And I resolve to invite Tom along to draft for me whenever he's available.

Just as I'm now better prepared to ride under windy conditions in the future, I'm better prepared if any of our kids come home to live with us again. Tom and I will welcome them not as kids in need of training, but as young adults in need of their own space.

I want our home to be a haven for them. A place they can count on for good food and rest. A temporary relief from the financial burden of paid housing. A stopping place on their journey.

Whenever our kids come home, I'll greet them. And when they leave again, I'll send them out with that old Irish blessing:

May the road rise to meet you.
May the wind be always at your back.
May the sun shine warm upon your face;
and the rains fall softly on your fields.
Until we meet again,
may God hold you in the palm of his hand.

TAKE FIVE! QUESTIONS FOR REFLECTION

Against the Wind: Return of the Fledgling

- Have your adult children returned home for a season? What surprises (positive or negative) did you face?

- Did you ever return home for an extended stay after you became an adult? Were there problems or issues between you and your parents?

- Are you willing to compromise in order to let your adult child have more freedom and independence? What are your non-negotiables?

- What are your biggest fears or concerns about your young adult child? Can you give them over to God?

- Are you willing to have a conversation with your adult child in order to come to a mutual agreement about expectations before they move back home?

CHAPTER 14

Reflections on an Autumn Ride

BIRDS ON THE WING

Tom checks his weather app. "This may be one of the last rides of the season. If we don't leave soon, we won't make it back before dark." He paces the floor as I fill up my water bottle and don my helmet.

In the fall, our rides become fewer and farther between. Cooler weather and shorter days limit our opportunities. We often want to get out and enjoy the gorgeous fall colors, but there seem to be more rainy days than sunny, and then, before we know it, most of the leaves have fallen.

As we hit the trail on this early October evening, I see the geese arranged in their perfect "V" formation, pointing southward. The wonders of God's creation amaze me. These winged creatures have the uncanny ability of knowing when to fly. And when to return home.

It's now been more than a year since Tom's accident and the emptying of our nest. As we ride, I remember the migration of our four offspring.

I was apprehensive about saying goodbye to our youngest and beginning our new journey of empty-nesting; of living together in the quiet spaces of our big, hollow home.

However, with all of our flitting about (i.e., traveling) and feathering, or de-feathering, our nest (i.e., uncluttering and redecorating), our lives were more active and full than I'd imagined. When the quietude filled our home, I didn't mind. It was a silence I'd longed for during the earlier chaotic years.

That first year passed in no time. When the school year ended, the young adults began arriving back home. First came Leah. My quiet, empty nest was buzzing again with the sounds of humming, piano playing, guitar strumming, laughter, and FaceTime conversations with friends. There were now three of us at the dinner table. And there was a soprano voice to accompany my alto in church on Sunday mornings.

Next came Chloe, who had survived her freshman year of college. We added several more plates to the table as she brought with her an endless stream of friends excited to reunite after a school year apart. The noise in our nest increased.

The crescendo grew as Jared, Seth, and Maddie swooped in for the Memorial Day weekend. Our table, and our hearts, were full.

As we sat at dinner that weekend with all my children chatting and eating together, I glanced out the window at our bird feeder. The grosbeaks flew happily about, also content to be back home in their familiar surroundings.

The rose-breasted grosbeaks appear on our backyard feeder like clockwork on the first of May. I can count on their appearance just as I count on the lush maple-leaf carpet over our lawn in October, the blanket of Michigan's lake-effect snow in January, and the green fingers of hostas pointing to the bright blue sky in April. I know the rosy-chinned males and their less-flashy female counterparts will show up because, in the twenty-plus years we've lived in this house in the woods, they always have.

Although most people say robins are the first sign of spring, for me, it's Mr. and Mrs. Grosbeak. When the temperatures rise in the north, and the daylight hours lengthen, they make their annual pilgrimage back home from Mexico or the Caribbean where they've been chasing bird-dreams and vacationing all winter long.

They locate their nesting ground somewhere in our woods and, together, they work to build a nest out of twigs, sticks, grass, and straw, followed by a soft lining of hair and other fine twigs. Mr. & Mrs. Grosbeak test it out to make sure it's a safe home for their eggs and fledglings.

During the summer, with their nest now empty, they flit about, defending the bird feeder from the other couples who encroach on their territory, and fill up on black-oil sunflower seeds. When autumn shows up with its shorter days and cool gentle rains falling on pumpkins, the couple catches a southward breeze and heads for the warmth of the rainforest.

But they'll wander back, given time. This is their home, where they've made little bird memories, found safety, and delighted in an abundance of seeds, flowers, and trees.

And so it is with my own. They fly away. Then they return.

Our children show up on different days, one by one, or all together. We can count on them to visit on special occasions—Mother's Day, Christmas Eve—or random weekends. They stay in the guest room or basement for a few days or weeks, or settle back into their old bedrooms for a summer. We expect them because this is home.

Our college students are learning to fly on their own. Their wings are still unsteady as they maneuver the strenuous currents of classes, finances, requirements, and romance. The elders coming from other parts of the country are seeking adventure, changing jobs, learning new skills, and finding (and sometimes losing) love. They're flying on their own and beginning to soar.

Chasing dreams can be exhausting, and eventually, the youngsters and the elders alike look toward home, a place where they can forget their troubles. They come with their bags, their laundry, their books, and their laptops. They come to rest.

They also come to reconnect with each other and their friends. They flit around the nest, upstairs and down, playing games, watching movies, making music, and laughing. Squabbles happen, too, but much less than when the nest was full of hatchlings, when they all lived together, all the time. They've learned to value their time together, as have I. These bonding times are now infrequent and precious.

Like our backyard friends, they come for food. For Mom's taco nights, spaghetti dinners, burgers on the grill, tortilla soup, and everyone's favorite—tuna noodle casserole! (Not kidding.)

They come for another kind of nourishment as well: for the love and support they know Tom and I provide. We listen while they share what's been going on with their jobs, their schooling, their boyfriends or girlfriends. They ask us questions and seek our advice as they make plans and dream dreams.

Eventually, it's time for them to set off again to chase those dreams. They load up their cars, or catch a bus or plane, and off they go. I know they'll come back, even if only for a day, to the home where a piece of their hearts remains.

Here, they find safety, acceptance, and love. Here, they are blessed.

With the crisp cool air biting my now-rosy cheeks, I follow Tom as he turns the corner toward home. Riding allows me to see the world at a slower pace and to soak in the subtleties of the changing seasons. I give thanks for the patterns of our lives—we go out and we come back home. Today, we come home to an empty nest.

I have to admit; I love the freedom and peacefulness we find there. But I won't complain when my nest fills up again. I'll never tire of the sound of birds chirping in my backyard trees, nor of my loved ones filling our empty rooms.

I look forward to when my little ones once again fly home and fill my nest with laughter, love, and joy.

Take Five! Questions for Reflection

Reflections on an Autumn Ride: Birds on the Wing

- How often do your adult children visit? Are you content with the frequency?

- What brings you joy when the children visit? What do you struggle with during your time together?

- How can you encourage family closeness when it's not possible to be together physically?

- How can you foster healthy relationships among your children?

- What traditions or memories do you cherish as a family? What makes them so special?

Part 4

CROSSING THE FINISH LINE AND REAPING THE REWARDS

CHAPTER 15

Mile Markers, Milestones, and Millstones

WHEN COMPARISON DRAGS US DOWN

As I pass mile marker #15, I hear someone behind me say, "Comin' around!" Seconds later, a pack of racing bikes zooms around me on the left. I call them "racing bikes" because, even though this isn't a race, they seem to be racing. They're moving so fast I can hear the whir of their wheels as they spin by me.

I'm so slow. What do they think of me?

With their sleek bikes and sleeker, athletic bodies, they must notice my not-so-sleek, overweight body as it struggles to move up the slightest incline. I beat myself up a little for not sticking to my low-carb diet over the past month.

The voice from my Cyclemeter app interrupts my thoughts. "Average speed, 13.45 miles per hour. Distance, fifteen miles. Total time . . ."

Did it say 13.45 miles per hour? That's pretty good! My usual speed range is between twelve and thirteen, so over thirteen means I'm moving along at a good clip, for me. I push the other bikers out of my mind and allow a burst of adrenaline to course through me on the approach to the next hill.

Forcing my legs to pump harder, I notice I'm closing in on two other lady bikers. I pump harder. "On your left!" I shout before easing past them. There's a shift in my thought process as I again compare myself to other bikers. This time I'm better. I'm winning!

But *this isn't a race*.

There's a fine line between healthy competition and unhealthy comparison.

In my younger days, I learned to compete through playing Mousetrap, Monopoly, and Masterpiece with my siblings. We had swimming races in the pool and contests to see who could hold their breath underwater the longest. In high school, I competed for first chair in the trumpet section and to get all gold medals at solo and ensemble contests.

My cousin and I were the same age. And even though we were best friends, we were also each other's biggest competitors. She was typically the winner. Like when she nudged me out of the salutatorian position by a nose. I said I was glad I was third in the class, because I didn't have to make a speech at graduation. But there was still a part of me that wished I'd beaten her.

Competition during my school years pushed me to be the best I could be. When my dad rewarded my achievements with praise, it drove me to set even higher goals. I wanted to win. At times, I did; other times, I didn't. Still, I achieved many of my goals, and I can thank competition for that.

As I grew older, there were fewer contests to compete in and competition turned into comparison. Especially in parenting.

Wow, we moms can compare! We compare feeding methods, cloth versus disposable diapers, and how soon and for how many hours our babies sleep through the night. As they grow, we compare their language development and academic achievements. Ultimately, we measure our own worth by how our kids' behaviors, skills, and successes compare with those of our friends' kids.

The problem with comparison is we become puffed up with pride when we compare ourselves favorably or are disappointed and insecure when we don't. Neither pride nor frustration is a healthy mental state. Still, I easily fell into the comparison trap as a young mom.

"Wa- tootie!!" two-year-old Chloe yelled.

I cringed as I imagined the sideways glances and raised eyebrows of my friends in the mom's group that met for coffee and Bible study every other Friday. When the kids came up from the basement playroom to join us for snacks, I listened closely and took mental notes.

Another two-year-old politely asked: "May I have a cookie, please?"

And another: "I like chocolate chip cookies. Mommy makes them at our house."

"Wa- tootie!!" Chloe repeated. I knew better than to make her perform and say "please" in front of my friends, so I quietly slipped her the cookie and sent her off to play.

Invariably, the conversation would turn to our children. As I chatted about my little ones, my voice was confident and self-assured. But underneath lurked the voice of uncertainty and shame. The voice of a mom who measured and compared and worried about whether her kids would achieve the "developmental milestones" we all knew were the gospel of child-rearing.

I heard my friends' toddlers speaking in articulate, mini-adult-like sentences, so eloquent they could join a toddler debate team. I compared them with my child's silence or garbled, dysfluent, one- or two-word utterances that were so unintelligible I was the only one who could understand them. And sometimes, even I had no clue.

I fretted about those developmental milestones. To make matters worse, as a practicing speech-language pathologist, I knew exactly how my kids measured up.

I'd memorized language development norms in grad school years before I had my own little ones. So understandably, as a new mom, I waited with great anticipation for those first words at one year; the 10-15-word count at eighteen months; and 50-100 words that included two-word combinations and a good mix of nouns and verbs at age two.

I did all the right things to promote on-target language development. I imitated their cooing and had "conversations" with them long before they had words, shaping their babbling into actual words and giving meaning to their vocal play.

"Mmmm," my little darling would innocently utter while munching on Cheerios in the highchair.

"Mmmmore? You want mmmmore?" I'd reply, also using baby sign language for "more" at least a half-dozen times before helping those little hands form the sign as well.

Later, during playtime, I'd hear "Bababa," from across the room.

Running to find a ball, I'd thrust it into those same tiny hands and say, "Ball! You want a ball!" My little one tossed it aside with disinterest.

As my babies grew into toddlers, I expanded those utterances, from one word to two, or two words to three or four. I was forever aiming for the next milestone of language development.

In my mind, with all of this spot-on language stimulation, my kids should definitely start talking early. After all, the norms were averages, right? And surely with all my know-how and targeted interaction, my kids should come in above average, somewhere to the right on that bell-shaped curve.

I might have been correct in my assumptions if it weren't for one important detail I neglected to consider. All of my knowledge and the many attempts to cultivate their speech could not change my children's genetics.

When I look at my kids now, it's obvious that all four have a similar genetic makeup. After all, they're the biological children of the same two people. Genetics gives them their natural tendencies toward music and math, both of which are strengths Tom and I brought to the table.

Yet, rather than focusing on those strengths, I stressed about the skills they didn't excel in, which, for all of them, included talking. Much to my chagrin, they did not talk early. Instead, they were pretty "average;" just barely hitting typical norms at expected ages.

In my opinion, that was too slow. I wanted them to speak in sentences at age two, like my friends' kids. I wanted to show my prowess as a language stimulator and a super-speech-pathologist-mom. My kids, however, showed me something different.

Eventually, I realized God had given each of my children, as well as my friends' children, their own unique gifts. My worry and angst stemmed from fear, insecurity, and envy. The milestones had become a millstone, dragging me down with the emotional burden of feeling as though neither I nor my children were measuring up.

Perhaps the greatest realization, though, was that my children were not talking *for* me. They were talking *to* me.

They had been talking, but I hadn't been listening. When I finally stopped measuring, comparing, and counting words, it freed me up to listen. And the circle of communication became clear and complete.

What mattered most was not where my children landed on that bell curve, but where their words landed when they tumbled out of their mouths.

Their words didn't need a measuring stick, but a listening ear.

They didn't exist to give me bragging rights, but to provide a bonding relationship.

They shouldn't be categorized as parts of speech, but captured by my heart.

Over the years, I loosened that millstone around my neck and accepted the developmental milestones for what they were: Averages. Guidelines. General markers to help parents along the way.

Children's words serve a higher purpose. They call us to listen, to understand, and to form relationships that will last long after they meet those milestones.

Sometimes it takes a few decades for these lessons to sink in.

I only wish my former self could have seen "future, talkative Chloe". If she had, she'd have laughed at the irony that her two-year-old, who couldn't pronounce "cookie," would someday work at a bakery to put herself through graduate school. And after a long day of event planning and marketing cookies, that child would come home to snuggle with her cat.

A cat that she just happened to name . . . Cookie.

Now that my kids are adults, I've completed a large part of my parenting job. My empty nest allows extra time for me to focus on my own goals and personal growth. This season of life and the freedom that comes with it pushes me to aim higher in my achievements.

Biking is one of those areas where I'm pushing myself and making progress. And yet, I still fall into the comparison trap. I shake my head as I remember the shame I felt at mile-marker #15, and then at the pride that surged through me as I passed those ladies on the uphill. Again, I remind myself: *This is not a race.* And I continue to pedal.

My nieces and nephews ran cross-country for years and I rarely heard how they placed after a race. I *did* hear, however, when they set a new PR, or Personal Record. They, their teammates, and their parents were thrilled! They taught me a PR was the best way to measure progress, set attainable goals, and be content with your own pace.

I'm trying to do just that—to stop competing and comparing and instead do my best given my situation and abilities. I'll improve as I'm able. And when I'm not at my best—if I slow down or miss the mark I'm shooting for, if my time or circumstances limit me, or if my aging body fails me—I can give myself grace.

Just as I learned to stop focusing on developmental milestones as a measure of my children's (and therefore *my*) success and worth, I'm learning to love the ride for the ride's sake. As I spy another rider in the distance, I choose to soak in the pleasure of movement, the high of accomplishment, and the satisfaction of self-acceptance.

TAKE FIVE! QUESTIONS FOR REFLECTION

Mile Markers, Milestones, and Millstones: When Comparison Drags Us Down

- When have you compared yourself to others? Did it result in a productive or nonproductive outcome?

- Can you think of a time when competition helped you achieve a goal?

- What drives you to compare yourself and your children with others?

- Why is comparison detrimental to ultimately meeting your goals?

- What goals have you set for yourself and how can you measure your success?

CHAPTER 16

Treasures from the Trail

RELECTIONS ON RESOURCEFULNESS

As Tom and I ride our bikes along the Migizi (mih-GEE-zee)—our favorite trail in Minnesota—tall oaks, birch, and pines provide refreshing shade on this scorching summer day. I'm struck by the beauty of filtered sunlight shimmering through the trees like fairy dust before alighting on wildflowers and tall grasses on the forest floor.

I stop every whipstitch to snap a photo of some hidden treasure. Even though my ride takes longer with these frequent, fleeting stops, I can't help myself. Wild red columbine, white daisies, and bluebells show off, gearing up for the Fourth of July, while wood sorrel with heart-shaped purple leaves huddle together in groups of three. In pine groves, the trees smell of Christmas, but stand in formation like the marching bands we watch in the fall.

Occasionally, a deer, just a few feet off the trail, stands motionless before darting away a split second before I can snap a picture. We sneak a peek at Pike Bay through the trees with its inviting blue waters. I can almost hear the waves lapping against the shore.

But that's not the water I hear.

Instead, it's the roar of the pressure washer in the driveway that has interrupted my daydreams of Pike Bay and the Migizi Trail. Tom has begun his annual task of cleaning the exterior of the house and I realize I also have work to do.

I'm not on a Minnesota trail. Nor am I on my bike.

On this sunny, fall Saturday morning, I'm at home in southwest Michigan and I have a huge to-do list of boring tasks like cleaning a carpet runner dotted with pee stains from our aging dog. Also on the agenda is listing junk (ahem, treasures) through online garage sales as we purge our house of its extra stuff. I wouldn't call it "death cleaning" just yet; I'll go with "downsize cleaning." Maybe someday we'll want a smaller place.

Still sipping my coffee and not ready to get to work, I gaze into the backyard from my comfy chair. The sunshine through the trees makes me think again of the Migizi Trail, and I wish I could take a ride. I want the sun on my shoulders and the wind on my face. Our empty nest usually gives us more time for biking, as we once dreamed it would.

We not only ride on vacation in Minnesota, but also hit the trails and roads around home in Michigan and Indiana. The previous week I'd biked my age in miles—a goal I hope to shoot for as long as my old bones allow. Building strength and endurance for biking requires hours of training and a flexible schedule—both of which were in short supply when the kids were home.

Still, a ride is not on today's agenda. And suddenly, my other to-do list items take a backseat also as I notice the sun struggling to reach me through the dirt and dust on my filthy windows. A hazy, dusty view of sunshine all winter long is unacceptable.

I retrieve the Windex and a stack of newspapers (Pro tip: Newsprint leaves fewer streaks) and begin the job I dread. It's not what I expected to do today, but sometimes the unexpected interrupts life. With the bottle of bright blue liquid cleaner in hand, I'm reminded of the lakes we visit over the summer, and my brain once again shifts back to Minnesota.

A few years earlier, I was riding the Migizi Trail with my sister, my niece, and Leah. Before the bike path enters the woods, it runs parallel to the highway. It's not our favorite part of the ride because of audible traffic and limited scenery, but on this day, it held a gift none of us expected.

We were almost to the woods when we heard an unusual sound over the noise of passing cars. Within seconds, we all put on our brakes to hear a tiny, but mighty, "Meow!" coming from deep in the bushes.

My sister is a cat lover. My niece is a cat lover. Leah is a cat lover.

Me? Not so much.

As the other three immediately began searching, I said, "Really? What are we going to do with a cat? We're on our bikes!"

"But what if it's hurt or starving? We can't just leave it here!" one of the cat lovers responded.

I rolled my eyes and considered riding on without them.

"Be careful! It's probably wild and has rabies," I said. Though I'm usually open to adventure, I don't believe in taking unnecessary risks. Reluctantly, I hung around to make sure no one got hurt.

"I can hear it, but I can't see it," Leah said as she scoured the bushes between the bike path and the highway. Finally, she found her treasure. "There it is! It's a kitten!"

I struggle to open the first window. I'm convinced an engineer with huge biceps designed them, as it takes superhuman strength to yank the windows from their seals to wash them. I rarely accomplish the job in a day, as I move from pane to pane, and eventually from pain (in my arms) to pain (in my back).

Typically, I get about half of the windows done before I give up for the day. Then it seems we don't have another good weather day when I'm free, so the other half wait until the next year. Today, though, the job invigorates me and I get through about 90 percent of the windows before my arms and back scream, "No more!"

Is it possible I'm getting stronger as I'm getting older? I might be. I'm also getting smarter, as I discover two new window-washing tricks that not only make my job easier but also more fun.

First, I sweet-talk Tom into spraying all the screens for me.

"Do you think you could maybe try to spray a screen?" I ask, tilting my head and raising my eyebrows.

Not one to miss an opportunity to continue to spray water on a warm, sunshiny day, he grins. "It's worth a try."

It works beautifully! Instead of brushing or vacuuming each screen, I carry them out to the driveway and let him play with his adult-sized water gun. When I come back later, they're drip-drying.

The second "trick" I discover is on the upstairs windows. Instead of struggling to pull all the windows to the inside, I climb a ladder and wash several outside on the porch roof in the sunlight. It's so much easier! I'm surprised this idea has never occurred to me before.

My sister, my niece, and I held our collective breaths as we watched Leah reach through the brambles and gently pull out the tiniest, fluffiest, most adorable, blue-eyed fur ball I'd ever seen!

So much for not being a cat lover. My practical side took flight as I opened up to the new cat-loving version of myself I hadn't even known was in there.

After discussing our options, we slid the helpless darling into Leah's neon-yellow string bag, which she carried on her back as we biked the remaining ten miles. We met Tom halfway around the trail. Shaking his head as he peered into the bag, he quickly gave up trying to argue any sense into us. By the time we finished our ride, we'd decided on the perfect name—Migizi.

I'm up to Leah's bedroom window now. As my hand moves in a circular motion across the glass, Migizi playfully bats at it from the inside. Standing on the roof, I see my home, and myself, from a new perspective. I was thirty-four years old when we had it built, and I'd never climbed on the porch roof until now. Had I been afraid to climb up on the roof? Or was I trapped inside by the constant needs of my busy household?

The windows are sparkling, and as the grime and dust disappear, I see my reflection. When did I become this middle-aged lady with crow's feet by her eyes and saggy cheeks? Where have the years gone?

Moving to the stairwell window, I remove the dirt and peer inside. I see eighteen years' worth of my kids' group portraits on the wall, reminding me of a busier time gone by. A time when I couldn't do this job without a thousand interruptions:

"Mom! Chloe won't leave me alone. Tell her to stop singing!"

"I was here first! Then Leah started playing the piano!"

"How many times do I have to tell you to *clean. Up. This. Room*?"

"Seth, you have homework! Turn off that video game and *get. To. Work*!"

"Is everybody ready? Get in the car! Jared's going to be late for his game!"

"I can't find my shoes!"

Today, though, it's quiet. There are no interruptions. No squabbles. No yelling. No soccer balls being kicked around.

I listen, but I hear no constant hum of the Mario theme song. No piano. No singing.

No kids.

Except for the periodic churning of the pressure washer on the other side of the house, it's just me, an aging dog inside asleep on a piece of smelly carpet, my windows, and the sunshine.

I'm by myself with no one to talk to. No one to laugh with. No one wanting to climb on the roof with me. Except Migizi—my buddy—now a big, fluffy three-year-old fur-ball. I don't blame him for wanting to join me in the sunshine on this new adventure.

Sometimes I miss that past life: the good, the bad, the laughter, and the tears. The noise of a nest that's full.

Sadness tries to cover me like a cloud, but the sunshine brightens my melancholy mood. It glimmers through the turning leaves as if to say, "You've got this. You're strong and brave, and you know how to find the bright side."

Getting older and emptying my nest isn't all that bad. It gives me peace and more time. Time to think, reflect, and be grateful. To get stronger, braver, and wiser. To wash 90 percent of my windows in one day. To become a cat lover.

I whisper a prayer of gratitude for the gifts of work and play. And for the sun that shines a light on all my hidden treasures.

TAKE FIVE! QUESTIONS FOR REFLECTION

Treasures from the Trail: Reflections on Resourcefulness

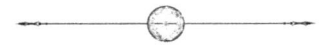

- What is the worst part of aging?

- Have you learned strategies for accepting the changes that come with age?

- What benefits of aging have you experienced?

- Has maturity brought stability and cooperation to your marriage? If so, how? If not, how might you encourage a sense of cooperation with your spouse?

- What surprises and "treasures" have you experienced with age?

.

CHAPTER 17

Like Riding a Bike, or Not

BRINGING BACK ADVENTURE AND SPONTANEITY

"We should go somewhere this weekend! I'm tired of sitting home all alone in this quiet house," I say to Tom, as we eat our dinner.

The winter had so far delivered ice storms, a polar vortex, heavy system snow, and lighter lake-effect snow (the big, fluffy flakes that blow off Lake Michigan). The school system I work for had used up ten snow days by mid-February. It had thrilled me to get those calls at five-thirty in the morning on days one through six when it was a welcome reprieve during the cold, dark winter doldrums.

I started getting a little antsy on days seven and eight. *How long was this going to last?* By days nine and ten, I was downright agitated. I'd not only watched all the new episodes of *Tidying Up with Marie Kondo* on Netflix, but I'd also Marie-Kondoed my closet, kitchen, and mudroom. After spending hours in my PJs, reading and writing, completing the girls' financial aid forms, drawing up meal plans, and catching up on other menial tasks I usually put off, I was running out of things to do. Or, at least, the desire to do them.

We finally returned to work and now it was hump day and Valentine's Day eve. It was also two days before our long Presidents' Day weekend break. I looked forward to spending more time at home almost as much as I yearned for that canned music playing on repeat when I'm put on hold at the doctor's office.

Tom and I had made a reservation at one of our favorite local restaurants for the day after Valentine's, since Friday was a better date night in our minds, and to avoid the holiday crowds. We had nothing else planned for our weekend. I could already foresee dreaded hours of Kondo-ing the bathroom closets and craft cabinets. Ugh. Cue the repetitive music.

"Well, I *do* have plenty of vacation time built up, and no meetings scheduled on Friday," Tom says after checking his calendar.

"Then it's settled! Where should we go?" I ask. We discuss all the usual suspects—Chicago, Indy, or maybe even farther south to escape the cold weather—before tabling our decision until the next day, so we can spend some time pondering our choices.

We're not the most spontaneous of travelers. We usually have our itinerary planned at least a couple of weeks or even months in advance. This last-minute, atypical adventure has me tingling with excitement.

The next evening, Tom walks through the door, drops his bags on the bench, and asks, "So, where are we going tomorrow?"

I'd been Googling and searching the VRBO, Airbnb, and hotel websites for a couple of hours. Over lunch, my co-workers had suggested Traverse City, Michigan. I took the idea and ran with it.

"Um, what do you think about Traverse City?" I ask with a sideways squint, not sure how he'll feel about driving four hours each way and heading north into what could be colder and snowier weather. He raises an eyebrow and cocks his head, but hears me out. "There are supposed to be great wineries and cute shops! And maybe we could even try some outdoor sport like cross-country skiing or snowshoeing. *Or* . . . fat-tire biking?"

I probably had him at *wineries,* but *biking* seals the deal. An interested grin creeps over his mouth and he agrees.

I cancel our Friday night dinner reservation and book a hotel instead, deciding on a Comfort Inn with good ratings and an even better price.

It seems the older we get, the more we enjoy our routines. That's commendable, especially when our routines and habits are healthy ones, like meditating, exercising, eating breakfast, and getting to bed on time. Still, there's something to be said for occasionally shaking things up, adding a little spice to our lives, and taking chances. Though fresh adventures can challenge our status quo, they can also broaden our experiences and help us discover unexpected rewards.

I took up knitting when my kids were younger and found it fascinating how my fingers—utterly tangled in the yarn when I began—soon moved in a smooth, perfect rhythm. I produced a lovely even row of knits and pearls, where once had been a tight, then loose, mess of unidentifiable stitches. Practice was the key.

That I could learn to knit later in life showed me our brains still have some plasticity. And since my mother suffered from Alzheimer's disease before her death, I've since paid attention to any new research regarding brain health. I've learned that novel, complex activities light up new synapses, keep the mind sharp, and decrease the chances of degeneration later in life. And so, when a new interest intrigues me or a challenge comes my way, I remind myself it's good to get out of my comfort zone.

When I resumed riding bikes with Tom during the kids' teenage years, I didn't think it would be much of a challenge. I'd learned to ride a two-wheeler as a kid, and that skill remained with me. The familiar adage "it's like riding a bike" implies that once you learn a skill, you'll never forget how to do it. But whoever coined the phrase likely hadn't experienced the vast differences between bicycles and riding styles. A whole new set of obstacles and challenges can arise, even when "riding a bike."

When I first mounted my new road bike with tires so thin they reminded me of the LPs I grew up dancing to, I wasn't sure this "fat-bottomed girl" could even balance on them, much less frequently say, "I want to ride my bicycle." The fear of falling, combined with a hard, narrow seat that was killing me (not) softly, had me yearning for my old comfy hybrid bike and questioning my decision to upgrade.

The starts and stops were klutzy and painful at first, but with practice, my brain formed new pathways and I learned to take off and stop with minimal effort. The confidence I gained and the thrill it eventually brought was worth the initial discomfort.

For at least the second time in my life, I'd mastered the skill of riding a bike. I couldn't imagine there was much more to learn in this realm.

Friday morning, we load up the car, set our GPS for Traverse City, and drive off. Other than getting there and back, we have no plan for how we'll spend our time over the next three days. Being spontaneous again, like a newlywed, kid-less couple, is definitely an empty-nest perk.

While Tom drives, I use my laptop and phone to research things to do, make a list of the most compelling wineries, find a few fat-tire bike rental shops, and Yelp the area's restaurants. I study the outdoor nature trails, check out some maps, and memorize the general geography of the bays and peninsulas. Then I remember this "cool" thing I'd seen on Facebook a couple of months earlier.

"Hey, how would you like to try one of these new-fangled igloo things?" I ask Tom. "They have them all over Michigan at brewpubs to get people to hang out during the winter. You can sit outside under twinkling lights and they're heated. They look so cool! Literally."

Brewpub igloos intrigues Tom, and since "new adventures" is the theme of the weekend, he agrees we should add it to our must-do list.

We head straight up Old Mission Peninsula to the Chateau Chantal winery, the first of three we plan to visit. Upon our arrival, I push the car door open against 25-30 mph winds and blowing snow, grabbing Tom's arm to help me get to the front door of the winery. Although it's frigid outside, the soft reds and crisp whites warm us from the inside out.

We enjoy refining our skills: sniffing the bouquet; tasting the pepper, chocolate, or raspberry on our taste buds; and distinguishing among oaken flavors. We also learn the best wines have "a good finish" that enables flavor to linger after a tasting is done.

With three wineries down (and nearly three sheets to the wind), we check into our hotel. To our surprise, the pool area and hot tub are overflowing with rambunctious youngsters and their parents. We decide to go out for dinner first and hit the hot tub later, after the kiddos have gone to bed. Hauling our bags up to our room, we stumble into a pack of little boys racing with hockey sticks through the hallway. As I dodge a puck, I mutter, "Looks like there's a hockey tournament in town."

I later confirm my observation when, after dinner, the hot tub resembles an extra-large can of sardines. The Comfort Inn (and likely several other hotels in the area) is full of miniature Gretzky-wannabes and their families. A flashback of us and our crew adding to the hotel mayhem during Jared's soccer tournaments in Indianapolis crosses my mind. I guess we've no right to complain. Still, it's a bit unexpected for our spontaneous, *romantic* weekend getaway.

We resolve to have a good time anyway, turn on the movie *La-La-Land*, and eventually drift off to sleep.

Our room is situated across the hall from a sizable window overlooking the pool area. At around eight-o'clock the next morning, as all the hockey players are gearing up and carb-loading at the hotel breakfast, I peer down at an empty hot tub and pool. We quickly don our swimsuits and go for a short soak to start the day.

This is the morning when our true adventuring begins. The first item on the agenda is a fat-tire bike ride. Since we bike all summer long and try to keep in shape over the winter, we don't anticipate any problems riding bikes with fat tires on snow. I mean, how hard could it be?

Moments before we arrive at Brick Wheels, they rent out their last bikes. We walk across the parking lot to McLain's. "Sorry guys," says the salesperson behind the counter. "We're all out. We'd be happy to sell you one, though,"

"Uh . . . no thanks. We're not ready to invest yet."

We head for the door, concerned our adventure might be dead on arrival. There's only one more shop we know of—Suttons Bay Bikes. I call ahead and put a couple of rentals on hold as we make the twenty-five minute drive north.

The guys behind the counter fit us for our bikes, and Tom asks, "So, where do you suggest a couple of beginners go for a good first ride?"

They recommend the trail at Leelanau State Park and hand us a map. When we ask for pointers for fat-tire biking and explain our cycling history, all we get is, "Hmm . . . if you're only used to road bikes, it'll be interesting." They pump up our tires, put a rack on the car, load up two bikes, hand us helmets, and tell us to have a good time.

I don't notice them snickering in the rearview mirror as we drive off.

As we mount the rented bikes and set off on a barely groomed single-track trail, we quickly discover that fat-tire biking is *not at all* similar to "riding a bike." I feel like a six-year-old learning to balance all over again. It takes all my strength to get the tires to grip the snow and move the bike. And if I don't move fast enough, the front tire sinks into the snow, turns sideways, and topples me over. Fortunately, we can't go more than about two miles an hour, and there are fresh, soft snowbanks on either side of the trail, making for a soft landing that's only painful when the bike frame smacks into our calves and thighs.

I push on, and notice that Tom (who's typically in better shape than I am) is also having trouble. To say our ride is "interesting" would be an understatement. The surrounding pine trees and snow-covered branches are beautiful, but it's hard to take in the beauty amid this extremely challenging ride. I can only go about fifty feet before either falling or stopping to prevent a tumble, after which I gasp for air, walk my bike up a tiny hill, and then get back on again to repeat the process.

I occasionally lie on the soft bed of snow and look up at the sky through the maze of branches until my breathing and heart rate return to a more normal rate, before taking on the arduous task of lifting my "fat" self and my fat-tire bike out of the snow. It's exhausting and a bit humiliating, being completely unprepared for this unfamiliar activity. My goal is simply to finish the ride before slamming into a tree or having a heart attack.

With more persistence than I've needed in a long time, I make it to the end of the 2.5-mile trail an hour-and-a-half later. Tom eventually finds his groove, so he rides a bit more, while I drop my spent body into the passenger seat of our car and dream of the hot tub back at the hotel. I conclude this new skill is going to take a *long* time for me to learn, *if* I ever try it again.

Back in Suttons Bay, we thank the shop guys for the bikes and the adventure. At that point, they share with us some pointers we could have used earlier. Like how you should find trails that are well-groomed and packed on your first time out, and how letting a little air out of the tires can make the ride easier in certain conditions. Luckily, some kind riders on the trail had already shared the less-air-in-the-tire-secret with us, so we gained a little, and I stress *a little*, more control as we rode along.

I make a note to myself: When tackling new ventures, take pointers from those with experience.

We spend the rest of our day relaxing and unwinding at a few more wineries on the Leelanau Peninsula, browsing cute little gift shops at the converted old State Hospital/Asylum, and enjoying a delectable Italian dinner at Pepe Nero's. It's our one real splurge meal of the weekend, topped off with a decadent chocolate dessert our server refers to as "heaven on a plate." It is.

Back at the hotel, we again find the pool and hot tub filled to the brim with bodies both big and little. I guess the hockey players' parents need a break after carrying duffle bags, sitting on bleachers, and chasing kids all day. Although *my* aching body wants those bubbles too, my mind and good sense say, "Nope. Not tonight."

We settle in for the evening and watch a documentary on the life and then-living legacy of Ruth Bader Ginsburg. RBG was one woman not afraid of a challenge and a person who achieved her dreams despite many obstacles. I look down at the half-dozen bruises on my legs and wince a little. That crazy fat-tire ride almost did me in.

We take it easy on our last day. Another morning hot-tub visit is just the ticket for my sore muscles. In the afternoon, we check "eat in an igloo" off our to-do list with lunch at the HopLot in Suttons Bay. We wander through gift shops in downtown Traverse City, including the Cherry Republic, where we taste chocolate-covered cherries, cherry salsa, and hard cherry cider.

We end our day by visiting a couple more wineries. Mari Vineyards on Old Mission Peninsula is our finale. Reminiscent of a castle that overlooks rows of now dormant grapevines and the bay, it's striking. We slowly sip Merlot until we drain the last bit from our glasses. The finish is perfect, allowing both sweetness and warmth to remain as we step outside and look toward the frozen bay. We imagine what the scene looks like in summer.

"We'll have to come back." I say, "with our own bikes!"

"Definitely," Tom agrees, casually leaning against a stone wall with a far-off look in his eyes.

I reach for his glove with my mitten-covered hand, lean in, and kiss him on the cheek. "Thanks for a good time. It was exactly what I needed."

It was, in fact, just what *we* needed. On this empty-nest journey, we are learning the comfort of familiarity, the joy of spontaneity, and the excitement of brand-new adventures. That weekend, we stepped out of our comfort zone to find a slice of life that taxed our abilities and tested our strength. It also satisfied our yearnings and tickled our taste buds.

And the finish? We both agreed. With lingering warmth and sweetness, it was perfect.

TAKE FIVE! QUESTIONS FOR REFLECTION

Like Riding a Bike, or Not: Bringing Back Adventure and Spontaneity

- Now that you have more time and freedom as an empty nester, what adventures are on your bucket list?

- Have you found any new gems for weekend getaways or other short vacations? Share your favorites.

- What novel activities have you considered trying? What fears or hesitations might stop you?

- Have you encountered any rough spots while pushing yourself out of your comfort zone?

- What is one new thing you have learned or tried since becoming an empty nester? If you have tried nothing new yet, commit to finding one thing in the near future!

CHAPTER 18

Dusty Frames and Rusty Chains

THE GREAT PAUSE

With spring's arrival, I hear a faint, almost forgotten voice in my head that says, *Wow! It's a beautiful day for a ride!*

I hesitate to ask my still-hurting husband to get my bike off the trainer in the basement and out to the garage, but when I do, he graciously responds. "I don't want you to stop riding because I can't!"

I click the helmet buckle under my chin, put on sunglasses, and turn on some tunes. Putting my feet on the pedals brings memories of past hardship and the promise of hope. I say a prayer asking God to restore Tom's health and to keep me safe on my ride.

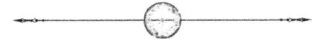

"I'm a fraud," I said as I stared at my blank computer screen. "How can I write a book about biking when we've hardly ridden all year?"

Tom shrugged as he limped by me. He was having another "bad back" day. Through his furrowed brow, I could sense frustration mingled with pain. Our bikes hung on their racks along the garage wall, gathering dust. Our helmets sitting atop the racks were now a cozy home for spiders spinning their webs. This was not the biking life we'd imagined. Once again, life had interrupted our ride.

Unlike Tom's previous bump in the road, this interruption was more of a wall. It forced us into a Great Pause. It lasted longer. Moved more slowly. And filled us with pain and grief.

Tom's history of back issues began a few years earlier, but his current back pain resulted from sitting in an unsupportive chair for too long while working from home one winter day. He'd been doing so well and then, without warning, that's all it took; now he struggled to walk as the pain radiated down one leg, making his toes tingle. He was doing everything he could—daily stretching, doctor visits, physical therapy—to fix his back before the spring riding season. But nothing seemed to help. It was an unwelcome interruption to our exercise life.

And then came the most unexpected interruption of all—Friday, March 13, 2020. The day the world shut down. None of us saw it coming. How could we? We'd never experienced a global pandemic before.

This is scary, I thought. *But if we all stay home and do as we're told, it'll be over in a few weeks. Right?*

So we did as we were told. Tom and I both began working from home. And our empty nest? It filled up faster than Costco's toilet paper stock emptied.

Leah was the first to come home. She had almost completed her fifth year of classes when the shift to online learning occurred. Now, each day, with textbooks and papers strewn across the basement floor and ottoman, she plopped onto the leather IKEA couch and opened her laptop for Zoom classes.

Chloe had been in the middle of a fabulous study abroad semester in Dublin, Ireland. Prior to her two-week spring break getaway to mainland Europe with new friends, we heard rumblings of several cities in Italy going into quarantine.

"I think you should re-route your trip, honey," I texted. "You don't want to go to Italy right now. They may not even let you in." She was disappointed to miss Rome and Venice but agreed it was the safest move.

One week into her spring break—after visits to Budapest, Bratislava, Vienna, and Salzburg—the museums and tourist sights closed down. The streets emptied and fear was setting in. She and her friends hopped on the first flight they could find back to Dublin, where she hoped to ride out the semester and this strange new threat known as "the novel Coronavirus." But when the number of cases in Ireland jumped from one to ten to sixty in a matter of days and the U.S. President started shutting borders and restricting international travel, her adventure was over. She was devastated.

After hours on hold with airlines to purchase tickets, a harrowing escape through crowded airports, and the obligatory two-week quarantine with a Dublin roommate after arriving back in the States, Chloe also made it home. Our nest was chirping with activity it hadn't seen in a few years.

We rearranged furniture, making office space for Tom in what had been my home office. I moved my space for providing online speech therapy and writing to our guest room. Chloe set up a classroom in her bedroom, Zooming to Ireland at all hours of the day and night.

There we were. No longer empty nesters, but working from home with no place to go, except the occasional grocery store run. I dusted off my sewing machine and started making face masks for the four of us. As spring sprouted up around us, our bikes were calling. Tom only went short distances before his back pain flared up. Without my partner to spur me on, I struggled to find the motivation to ride.

So the dust gathered.

Keeping a safe social distance and wearing masks, the girls and I made a quick trip to my parents' house to help my dad plant his garden. It was a novel experience for the girls that filled them with a new appreciation for manual labor. They looked forward to the promise of seeing their hard work come to fruition as green beans, cucumbers, tomatoes, and sweet potatoes at harvest time.

We took on an attic project with zest. Our storage area over the garage had become a mountain of boxes, luggage, bags of clothes to be donated, and the kids' old toys and memorabilia. After almost a week of purging, sorting, breaking down boxes for recycling, assembling new metal storage shelves, and organizing, we walked into the attic with a grand sense of accomplishment. There was now a place for everything, with everything in its place.

Near the end of May, we received the call we'd been waiting for with great anticipation. Our daughter-in-law had gone into labor, and in a few brief hours, God blessed us with the gift of our first grandson. It thrilled Seth and Maddie to become first-time parents, and for Tom and me, the title of "grandparent" was a long-awaited dream. Born amid a pandemic, our newest family member was the miracle we all needed.

Visiting our new arrival was a bit more challenging, but with warm weather, outdoor spaces, and masks, we made it work. We tickled his tiny toes, let his hands grasp our fingers, and laughed at every grimace, grin, and gas release. Our newest family member was a welcome intrusion to the Great Pause.

Classes wrapped up for the girls. My work also ended as that most unusual school year came to a close. Summer came, and with it, our annual vacation to Minnesota. We dusted off the bikes and hoisted them onto the rack. Since we'd hardly been riding at home, we weren't sure it was even worth the trouble. But those up-north trails are our favorites, and we couldn't miss them entirely. Our Minnesota days wouldn't be the same without at least a few bike rides.

But this strange pandemic year continued to refuse to be "the same" anyway. At the beginning of our second week at the lake, my sister and I received a worrying text. Our eighty-six-year-old father had fallen. At first, I envisioned a broken hip, but soon learned he'd hit his head and wasn't feeling well. The next text told us he'd become unresponsive. An ambulance was taking him to the hospital.

Our day of fishing and gift-shop browsing turned into shock and grief the moment we received that call from our oldest sister.

"He's not going to make it," she said. "The tests show a brain bleed, and it's too severe to stop. There's nothing that can be done."

At that point, the only thing keeping Dad alive was the respirator and his pacemaker. We said our goodbyes virtually before they shut everything down that evening. Our family's life had drastically changed in a matter of twelve hours.

In what seemed like a surreal experience, we spent the rest of the week at the cabin planning Dad's funeral. Sitting on our screen porch overlooking the lake in which Dad had loved to fish, my youngest sister and I FaceTimed with our two older sisters and brother at home. While discussing funeral plans, we also wondered aloud what we were going to do about Mom. Dad had been her primary caregiver for the past five years. At her stage of Alzheimer's, her short-term memory was nearly nonexistent. Dad's death had confused her even more, and she asked where he was every few minutes. She seemed to know something was wrong, but couldn't remember what had happened.

After returning home from the lake, we held Dad's funeral, complete with most of his seventeen grandchildren singing "Great is Thy Faithfulness," one of his favorite hymns. Then my siblings and I gathered around the table for a first of many meetings. Since Mom needed someone nearly 24/7, we put together a schedule of who could stay with her over the next few weeks while we researched long-term care solutions.

The pandemic had morphed into a time of grieving and caregiving. I spent days at a time with Mom, all the while answering her repeated questions of "Where's your dad?" "Have we heard anything yet?" "Did he die?" "How did he die?" And the hardest of all, "What am I going to do?" She felt lost without him. We all did.

I sorted through Dad's closet and dresser drawers, piling up shirts and pants for the charity thrift store. We picked beans and tomatoes from the garden that my girls had helped to plant. My siblings and I interviewed caregivers. When we met Lou, a former RN in her native country of the Philippines, we knew we'd found a gem. She moved into Mom's guest room shortly before school restarted for me and the girls.

Our nest emptied again for a few months as Leah and Chloe returned to in-person learning. My focus shifted back to COVID accommodations and restrictions, and, with the school's combination of in-person and virtual learning, my days were long. I learned a new protocol for delivering speech therapy that included clear masks, disinfection, and many virtual sessions. Nothing was the same anymore.

Leaving for work each morning and returning each evening through the garage, I saw our bikes hanging on the wall, staring at me through darkened headlights and taillights. Tom's back issues had worsened despite more doctor visits, MRIs, chiropractic treatments, and cortisone shots. The possibility of surgery was growing.

I took an occasional ride out of guilt on weekends, but without Tom to encourage me, it was hard to find the time or motivation to get on the bike. Most weekends I visited Mom, who lived nearly two hours south, or my new grandbaby, two hours to the north. If I wasn't off driving and visiting, I was catching up on neglected housecleaning, a result of long work hours and sheer exhaustion. When the weather turned cooler, Tom moved my bike to the basement trainer, where it saw even less action and more dust.

At the end of October 2020, that Great Pause morphed into a Great Wait. Mom's physical condition had been worsening for a few months and Lou insisted we take her in for blood tests. She was too weak to get out of bed, so again we watched as the EMTs lifted one of our parents into an ambulance to be taken to the hospital.

Tests revealed internal bleeding caused by stomach ulcers. Further tests revealed those ulcers were cancerous. With Mom's declining mental status, her weak physical condition, and the recent loss of her life partner, we knew that cancer treatment was something neither she nor Dad would have wanted.

As the lovely colors of October shifted into a cold and dreary November, we enrolled Mom in hospice care. She remained at home, which allowed us all to visit her despite the raging pandemic. And thus began the Great Wait.

Over the next five months, we visited and talked and laughed and cried. I held Mom's hands. When several of my siblings and I suffered mild bouts of COVID, there was quarantine and isolation. Throughout it all, we watched the devastating news of case counts, economic woes, and death tolls, and suffered through a contentious election. We canceled our annual extended family Christmas gatherings.

Tom continued to fight intermittent back pain, and a new malady caused by a knee injury. He was forced to give up any exercise, something he so loved and craved, that it caused him to struggle with his purpose in life and to question why God sends suffering. He shared these thoughts in our annual family review at Christmas time:

The disappointment and frustration through all of this have been palpable. It made it hard to focus on anything but my own issues. And yet the timing coincided almost directly with the ongoing pandemic and its devastation. I knew many were hurting and I certainly could relate. I became thankful for the things I could do, while still longing for those I could not. For me, the physical pain paralleled the societal pain all around me. What has gotten me through is God's grace. I know he's been with me. Whether in pain or in disappointment, I know he'll see me through to the other side of this. Just as he'll see us all through to the other side of the pandemic.

To our surprise, Mom rallied after Christmas, and we hoped a miracle was taking place. But after a few weeks of spunk and spirit, she again experienced fatigue and little appetite. The few bites of food she took each day did nothing to nourish her body; she shrank before our eyes.

When Lou needed time off or had to quarantine herself, we had the opportunity—the gift—to step in and care for Mom. I was grateful for each snarky comment she made, for each smile she graced us with, and for another day of life with Mom.

Shortly after the one-year anniversary of the beginning of the pandemic, around the ides of March, our hospice nurse said it wouldn't be long. Mom had stopped taking almost all forms of nutrition and hydration. She barely responded when she saw us and her smile had vanished, along with the gleam in her eyes. My siblings and I, and some of our spouses, gathered together at her bedside for last goodbyes. On March 31, my mother's soul left her body and flew away into the arms of Jesus. She and Dad were together again. The Great Wait was over.

At the second family funeral service in nine months, we celebrated Mom's life. Our long-distance kids, Jared and Chloe, flew home for a long weekend. Seth, Maddie, and our grandson drove down to be with us. Leah had already moved back home for her last semester and internship. Despite the sadness, having all our children together at home on Easter Sunday, the day before Mom's funeral, was a gift that brought me deep joy. And celebrating our Lord's resurrection was the reminder we needed that, for those who believe, death does not have the final say.

In the following weeks, we celebrated getting vaccines. News reports showed dropping case numbers and declining death tolls. In our own family, we celebrated Leah's graduation after six long years of school, followed by our grandson's first birthday, and then Chloe's graduation from college as well. It seemed the clouds of grief were finally dissipating.

As the wind caresses my face on this lovely spring ride, I reflect on the Great Pause that resulted in our necessary break from riding. Although the dusty frames and rusty chains were a sign that biking had taken a back seat, the rest of life still offered much to be grateful for.

Sprinkled throughout that year of grief and pain were times of immeasurable joy. Our grandson's arrival provided much laughter and many moments of wonder at his growth and development. The girls' return home for extended periods allowed us to discover the lovely young adults they'd become as we spent time together cooking, going for walks, or hanging out watching Netflix. Celebrating my parents' lives, and the many ways they'd enriched ours, strengthened bonds with our extended family.

I thank God for all the seasons of our lives. Through ever changing ups and downs, starts and stops, gains and losses, we have his loving arms to hold us up, push us on, and embrace us on the journey.

Take Five! Questions for Reflection

Dusty Frames and Rusty Chains: The Great Pause

- How did your life, marriage, or family situation change during the Great Pause (i.e., the COVID pandemic)?

- When life brings interruptions, how do you cope with pain, grief, or suffering? Where have you found sources of strength?

- What adjustments have you had to make to routines, schedules, or habits because of unexpected circumstances? How do these adjustments affect your state of mind?

- Are there ways you've learned to support your spouse or children during unexpected/unwanted events or struggles?

- Can you see points of light or moments of joy that resulted from, or that happened despite, these difficulties?

CHAPTER 19

The Trike

A NEW PERSPECTIVE

A couple of miles in, I ask Tom, "How's it going?"

"Not bad," he says. "I've definitely got a new perspective from here!"

"How's that?" I ask.

"I'm looking up and all I see are trees and sky!"

I think to myself that "road bikes" are aptly named. As you ride along in your most comfortable, neck-neutral position, you stare at . . . the road. Designed for smooth pavement, a road bike has narrow tires and ram's horn handlebars that force your eyes to stay focused on the pavement.

You take in the cracks and crevices, potholes, roadkill, and other obstacles. To see what's out in front, you angle your spine at the neck as far back as it can comfortably go. Then you're aware of road signs, other riders, and oncoming traffic. When the ride is calm, you glance left and right at your surroundings to take in the lush green cornfields, late summer wildflowers, and neighbors' front porches. After a minute, your neck muscles tighten and you look down again.

Over time, I've gotten used to it and haven't given it a second thought. Until today. Now I know there *is* another way and my husband is the one showing me.

When Tom turned sixty—I wasn't far behind—we heard all the familiar quips and jabs.

"It's all downhill from here." "Are you feeling washed up?" "How's the view from over the hill?"

And these, from his birthday cards:

"You're not old, you're vintage. (Okay, you're old too.)"

"Why party when you can nap?"

Except for the palatable pleasure of a "vintage" bottle of wine, none of these images of aging excite us. In fact, they mirror the way we often feel about the aches, pains, and general fatigue that comes with getting older.

We cringe at the thought of growing old, but there's no denying parts of us are already fading. We yearn for our younger selves when we had flexibility, energy, strength, physique, and wrinkle-free skin.

Like it or not, we are looking down that proverbial "hill." And like the typical posture on a road bike—looking down at wheels and the path—it robs us of the surrounding beauty. An aging body's degeneration keeps us focused on ourselves and our problems.

Unable to bike because of his enduring back pain, Tom, nevertheless, couldn't shake his desire to hit the trail. After missing nearly a year of cycling, he approached me with an idea.

"I've been doing a little research on recumbents," he said. "They're pricey, but if I started with a used one or a simpler model, do you think we could fit it into the budget?"

Recumbents, he explained, allow the rider to sit back rather than lean forward, taking the strain off of the spine. I was in favor of anything that might spark some joy back into his life. "We'll make it work. Let's check 'em out!"

The hunt was on. Like everything else during the pandemic, bicycles (including the recumbent style), were in short supply. We drove a couple of hours west to Chicago to test-ride some recumbent two-wheelers. They were awkward and required a whole new way to balance with Tom's feet on the pedals out in front of him. After two or three wipeouts on his test rides, I nixed them.

"You don't need another injury. A crushed elbow, bad back, and twisted knee are enough! Let's look at trikes instead." We'd read about the three-wheeled recumbent style—a conglomeration of gears, wheels, and seemingly endless chain—and the popularity it had been gaining over recent years, especially in *our* age group.

Not to be confused with amphibious baby frogs, the most common style of recumbent trike is the "tadpole," with two wheels in front and one in back. Tadpole trikes have bragging rights for being more stable than their two-wheeled predecessors. After test-riding one near home, Tom was hooked and inquired about purchasing it.

"Sorry, this one is spoken for," the shop owner told him.

"How long would it take to order one?" Tom fished his phone out of his pocket to look at the calendar. We had less than a month until our Minnesota vacation in July.

"Six to eight weeks, minimum," the man said. "There's no guarantee with the supply chain issues these days."

Tom's face fell. "Sorry, but that's too late. Thanks for your time anyway."

"We just have to keep looking. If it's meant to be, it'll be," I said as we headed to the car.

Back at home, Tom sat at his computer and started searching. A few days later, he finally found a trike in Dearborn, Michigan.

"Can you hold it for me until Friday?" I heard him ask. "Great! We'll be there by mid-afternoon."

It was a three-hour drive east, so we made a day of it. We put my bike on the rack and packed our helmets and other gear, hoping to get in a brief ride before coming home. Our future was looking up.

At the recumbent bike shop, the crew fitted him for his new wheels while I browsed around, taking in the unusual shapes and sizes of these awkward machines. Tom asked the usual plethora of questions and looked over every feature on his new ride. As he bounced from foot to foot, unable to contain his energy, I could sense his excitement at the prospect of riding again. The roadblocks he'd encountered over the past year and a half were being removed.

Still, there were hurdles to jump. For starters, we needed a means to transport this mammoth tadpole. Because Tom bought a folding model, it *could* fit inside our mid-size SUV, but it filled most of the car, leaving no room for luggage or backseat passengers. We already owned one bike rack, designed for two-wheelers, so investing in a new rack that would fit his trike *and* my bike seemed extravagant.

Once we were home, Tom devised a way to get his three-wheeler on our current rack alongside my bike. He thought it would work best if he removed the rear wheel, which we later learned was unnecessary. We also discovered putting said wheel back on was not a simple task. As he pushed, pulled, and finagled what seemed like a thirty-foot-long bike chain, I heard a "snap," followed by a string of expletives. The trike, which had taken miles of searching and weeks to find, had broken within the first twelve hours of ownership.

There have only been a few times in our marriage when I can say Tom lost it. This was one of them. He raged and paced in circles around the garage with his hands on his head, screaming, "I can't believe I just did that! Oh, my gosh! What am I going to do?" He uttered a few more choice words over the next few minutes before he finally cooled off enough to let me help him get the trike in the back of the car.

We headed off to our local bike shop even though we figured the chances of them having a random little piece for a foreign-made recumbent tricycle during a pandemic were slim. Thankfully, we figured wrong. They had the part and within a couple of hours, for a nominal cost, Tom and his trike were back in business.

Our rack-hack worked like a charm and a week later, we arrived safely in Minnesota, bikes on board. Tom was eager to get out for his first ride on the Migizi trail. Since a recumbent trike uses different muscles than a bicycle, he knew he wouldn't be able to ride the entire seventeen-mile loop his first time out. He also knew that trail better than some of our trails at home, as he rides it several times a year. He mapped it out and decided we would start at the campground near a more picturesque part of the trail.

With our luggage out of the car, he removed his bike seat, folded up the trike, and put it inside the car while strapping mine to the rack. The process took at least 20 minutes. Getting ready for his ride was already way more time-consuming and hassle-laden than jumping on a two-wheeler and taking off. The excitement I'd sensed in Tom at the bike shop only days before was morphing into frustration. But he persisted.

Was it going to work for him in the long run? This newfangled approach to biking was a lot of monkey business for a simple ride. As we drove along the washboard gravel road to the campground, leaving a wake of dust behind, we voiced our concerns.

"I sure hope this decision pays off," he said.

Glancing his way, I drew my breath in. "I'm beginning to wonder."

Arriving at our start point, we unloaded our bikes, unfolded the trike, reattached the seat, put on our helmets, and applied bug spray. It was finally time to ride!

I glance ahead at Tom on his recumbent bike. He looks comfortable—sitting in a reclined position, taking in his surroundings. I admit I'm envious. The trees on the Migizi trail are my favorite. From the white birch flanking our pathway to the tall pines reaching for the heavens, the trees remind me of God's presence in each present moment, his power reaching far beyond the pedals and predicaments we're so focused on.

I can look up at the trees for a moment here or a few seconds there, but I have to crane my neck to do so. Tom, on the other hand, has the freedom throughout his ride to soak in the azure skies and downy clouds beyond the prickly needles of the pines from an easy, relaxed stance. His new perspective allows a vantage point he'd missed on previous journeys.

Getting older can be a nuisance. Hassles and frustrations can derail our hopes and dreams. We spend our time circumventing roadblocks, only to face more hurdles.

Thankfully, getting older also offers an ever-widening viewpoint. As our lives and responsibilities change, we spend less time staring down at the road and more time sitting back, looking up, and taking in those awe-inspiring views.

As I pedal along, the song **"People Get Old"**[1] plays from my bluetooth speaker. I look around at the glorious scenery and sing along, the lyrics reminding me to be grateful for the passing years and the genuine gift of living long enough to get old.

TAKE FIVE! QUESTIONS FOR REFLECTION

The Trike: A New Perspective

- How has aging affected you personally? What do you find the most frustrating or difficult as you age?

- Have you lost the ability or ease to do something you previously enjoyed?

- What are your fears about aging? What can you do to overcome them?

- Has aging changed your perspective on life, love, family relationships, or God? If so, how?

- What joys have you found with age and how can you spread that joy to others (e.g., your spouse, friends, children, etc.)?

Chapter 20

Going the Distance

Promises to Keep

After years of increasingly long bike rides, Tom announces his plan to sign up for the Apple Cider Century (ACC). Drawing thousands of bikers from the Midwest and beyond, the ACC in Three Oaks, Michigan is a 100-mile ride that has been his goal for years. It's finally time to go the distance.

"So, you think you can do it?" I ask.

"I do," is his sure reply.

I've heard those words and seen that commitment before. I know he means it.

"I do."

Those two words have carried more weight than most others we've said in our lifetimes. We said them as we stood before a congregation of friends and family, surrounded by our wedding party in shades of ivory and peach, with the smell of tulips and roses awakening all our senses on that windy April day.

I was wearing the "Yes Dress" of the late '80s, featuring candlelight ivory lace and beads, puffed sleeves, plunging V-neck and a long, flowing train. Tom stood beside me in his ivory tux with tails, bowtie, and white-rosebud boutonniere.

The pastor asked if I took Tom to be my husband.

"I do," I said, my voice shaky with excitement, nerves, and emotion.

Then he asked Tom, "Do you take Linda to be your lawfully wedded wife?"

"I do," he said. "As long as we both shall live."

We'd prepared ourselves for this day and looked forward to going the distance.

But at twenty-five and twenty-six-years old, we had no idea how much ground we would have to cover. We didn't know about detours, storms, and bumps in the road we would face.

We were young, recent college graduates and lost in love. It was just the two of us "DINKs" (Dual-Income-No-Kids), as our friends called us, ready to embark on our carefree lives together.

During those three DINK years, we bought our first home, painted the bedroom with the same trendy pastel peach we'd used in our wedding, and replaced brown shag carpeting in the family room with a neutral-colored Berber. We took our first camping trip—making love in a tent on the shores of Lake Erie, the pounding of waves drowning out the rhapsody of our passion.

We dreamed of having kids someday but heeded the advice of friends who warned us our lives would never be the same. "Enjoy your couple-time together now. Once you have kids, things are gonna change!" And so we waited. Like two souls winding their way through the tunnel of love on a journey of joy, we were young and free!

We had three blissful years of marriage without children. Oh, there were typical newlywed arguments over housework and money—who's doing or spending more (or less)? We shared fears and tears as we worked out the insecurities and nuances of living together. But after three years of working out the bugs, a discussion about children came up again. We asked each other, "Do you want to try now?"

"I do" was again the answer. Both nervous and excited, we knew kids would change our lives. That baby-story had played out several times with our five nieces and the children of close friends. We knew the drill. Or so we thought.

We looked forward to having a cute little bundle of joy and being showered by friends and family with gifts and attention for having taken the plunge into parenthood.

I presumed having kids meant hours of endless entertainment, snuggles, hugs, and slobbery kisses. I imagined dressing up my real-life baby dolls in soft blues or pinks and parading them around the block in a stroller as I'd seen my neighbors do. I pictured singing my little one to sleep at night with a gentle lullaby.

Did I ever imagine it would take more than a lullaby to get those babies to fall asleep? Did I ever expect our sleepless nights would make us walk and work like zombies for the first several months? I did not.

Did I know we'd spend more time tying shoes, buckling car seats, cleaning up vomit, fixing broken toys, sorting clothes, kissing boo-boos, helping with homework, attending concerts, watching recitals, cheering at sporting events, and driving (so much driving!) than we'd likely spend at our jobs over the next two decades? I did not.

Could I imagine my heart would feel as if it would explode with love for these little humans Tom and I brought into the world? I could not.

And could I fathom someday those little humans would grow up and leave us? That we would be so proud and so broken all at once when they walked toward their college dormitory—their new home? I could not.

When Tom and I said "I do," we didn't know what we were doing. But we promised that whatever marriage and future parenting required, we would do it together.

Tom's passion for biking is one he was willing to share with me. Even while we were dating, the exhilaration of biking drew me in—not with the same fervor as Tom, but enough to persuade me to join his adventures. We often rode near our home and on vacations during those "DINK" years, but soon after our fourth child was born, it became such a production that we put biking on hold. Every night and day were, instead, filled with diapering, disciplining, and (have I mentioned?) so much driving. Parenting replaced pedaling as children became the center of our world.

By the time our boys went off to college and the girls were in their teens, Tom had found little windows of time to slip in a ride. As he'd done in the early years of our marriage, he urged me to join him, and so, occasionally, we would take a short ride together on a summer evening or weekend afternoon.

The year Chloe turned fifteen, Tom bought a new bike and enjoyed riding even more. Two years later, he convinced me to do the same. My new bike was easier on my old joints and tired muscles, which renewed enjoyment of the sport.

Life was good. Biking was good. Everything felt, oh, so good.

But life isn't always good. Getting it done in a marriage means hanging in there when the road isn't so smooth; to put our own needs aside and be there for each other.

After the fall that tore my rotator cuff, I needed help with everything from making dinner and driving the kids around to washing my hair and fastening my bra. Regardless of the task, Tom stepped in when I needed him. I did likewise for him after the bike accident that crushed his elbow.

The care we gave each other during those "bumpy" times reminded us of our parents' marriages. Tom's mom had modeled for us what genuine commitment looks like, as she cared for his dad until he passed away. Even though his confusion and memory loss made Tom's dad feisty and fitful, Mom could calm him down. My father-in-law knew as long as she was there at his side, he was going to be okay.

In a similar way, I saw my dad step in when Mom received her Alzheimer's diagnosis. When his wife of sixty years could no longer cook a meal or follow a recipe, this farmer, who primarily knew the way around his cornfields, learned his way around the kitchen. When Mom could no longer clean the house, Dad hired a home helper. When she couldn't remember what she'd just been told, Dad, though exasperated, repeated himself over and over (and over and over . . .) again.

Through observing our parents, we learned what it meant to be in it for the long haul. To push petty grievances aside and forgive imperfections. To embrace each other through grief, sadness, illness, and injury. We simply followed their lead.

Tom's excitement for the century ride is contagious and I decide to ride part of it, too. Our training begins in early spring before blossoms even appear on the apple trees. By the last Sunday in September, after apples have been picked, and cider pressed from them, we mount our bikes amid the other cyclists. My goal is to ride 100 kilometers, about 62 miles. His goal is the full 100 miles. We are going the distance. With the wind at our backs and the sun shining warm on our faces, nothing can stop us.

Indeed, we both achieve our goals that day. Tom's sense of accomplishment in crossing that finish line after 100 miles sends him right back into training the next spring and summer, as his new goal is to ride at least one century a year. Little does he know, he'll hit that bump in the road that will throw him off his bike, throw him off course on the way to his second century, and throw our lives into upheaval.

For better, for worse. In sickness and in health, so long as we both shall live.

Life has thrown us curveballs before. Babies with colic. Car accidents. Job changes. Children with attention deficits, scoliosis, and diabetes. Losing loved ones.

We lavish in the "for better" and "in health" times, but it's the "for worse" and "in sickness" times that remind us our vows were for *all the times*. Riding with our partner at our side has gotten us over many bumps along the way. Reminiscent of the words of a song we've played many times, "no one does '**(I do) like we do**.'"[1] And so, we persevere.

The year after the accident, Tom successfully completes a half-century despite the nerve pain and discomfort that beat him down on long rides. And the year after that, three years after his first century, he's finally ready to conquer the full distance again. I join him, hoping to set a personal record with three-quarters of a century.

We've trained and are ready to go. Remembering the sunshine of our first ACC, we look forward to a beautiful day and a smooth ride. Instead, the day dawns with the worst rainy-day forecast imaginable! Still, we're determined to cross that finish line. Tom fights hard to ignore his residual nerve pain, as well as his rain-soaked clothing and gear. He has promised himself he won't give up.

We both cross the finish line and taste of the thrill of personal victory. We said we would do it and we did!

So goes our life together. We keep the ultimate finish line in the back of our minds, not knowing when or where it'll be. But knowing we'll be at each other's side as long as our lives allow.

Now that we're older, wiser, and a bit worse for wear, we can look back over the days, months, and years that have passed and say with confidence that our "I do" truly became "I did."

Over and over (and over and over . . .) again.

Take Five! Questions for Reflection

Going the Distance: Promises to Keep

- Do you remember your wedding vows? What parts stand out in your memory?

- Think about your wedding day. How were you different then, from who you are now?

- What struggles did you face during the early years of your marriage?

- What difficulties have you faced later in your marriage?

- Why is making a lifetime commitment a scary thing? What is the greatest joy in making that commitment?

CHAPTER 21

A Race Against the Sunset

TIME TO SLOW OUR RIDE

I look at my phone's weather app and see the sun will set at 8:16 p.m. If I quickly change into my biking garb and hit the road, I can get twenty miles in before dark.

I'm on my own tonight since Tom has already completed his ride. I'd planned to skip exercising today until I stepped outside and noticed the mild temperature and lack of wind. The perfect riding conditions nudge me on, despite the setting sun and waning daylight.

One of the earliest chapters of our lives together involved a sunset.

I was pretty sure he was going to pop the question soon.

We'd been dating for only seven months, but our relationship had already grown into one of deep love and commitment. We were in our mid-twenties and by this point knew what we wanted in life—and in a partner.

That summer, shortly after I graduated from Purdue with my master's degree and began my job search, Tom signed up for two organized bike trips to Nova Scotia and New England. His adventures separated us for nearly four weeks, and that separation brought clarity. Out on the road with time to think, all the while missing his girl at home, Tom decided to make his move. When he told me he wanted to look at rings together, I knew we'd moved beyond "talking" about a future together. The big event was going to happen.

I was beyond excited. I was also a nervous wreck. When we were together, I fired questions at him.

"When are we going to do this thing?" I asked, wringing my bare fingers together.

"I've got a plan." Of course he did.

"Can you give me a hint?"

"You don't need to worry about it." I did anyway.

I wanted to be prepared when the moment came. I should look nice and be on my best behavior. What if I started an argument with him just before he'd planned for the big event to happen, and I ruined the moment?

He knew I was going crazy with uncertainty. He assured me it wouldn't be long.

In mid-July, he joined me on my family's annual fishing trip to Minnesota, a rite of passage my two brothers-in-law had already endured. A newcomer wasn't required to become a die-hard fisherman, but he should at least show an appreciation for the family tradition and laugh at the jokes during evening coffee time with the aunts and uncles. Would Tom pass muster?

Dad took us out fishing on the lake. Tom wasn't exactly hooked, but he showed the capacity to learn and kept an open mind. When we took a canoe out together, Tom got out and pulled the canoe through the water that was too shallow for paddling, while I rode in the boat like an Egyptian princess on the Nile. During our first long bike ride together—to Inspiration Peak—he was patient as I pedaled along behind him, and he frequently waited for me to catch up.

At the midway point of that ride, we stopped for a picnic lunch. Propping up my small digital Canon camera at one end of the wooden picnic table, I set the self-timer, ran to the other end of the table, and leaned in with a smile toward Tom. *Snap.* We forever captured the memory on film and in my mind.

He was passing the test. So far, so good. But what about that ring? I was about to burst. Was the big event going to happen here, away from home? Or did he plan to draw it out until he was back on his own turf?

It was Thursday afternoon when he suggested we go watch the sunset over a lake somewhere. Sounded pretty suspicious to me, but I tried not to get my hopes up. Still, I wore my favorite pastel blue cotton sweater, put on some makeup, and checked that my hair was looking good. Just in case.

We looked at a map and selected West Lost Lake since it was nearby. Even its name had a romantic "ring" to it.

A little before sunset, we hopped in the car and headed west. That's when we discovered our potential problem. The sun was setting too fast! In the late-1980s, there were no Internet or weather apps that could tell you the exact time the sun would set. Unless you had a *Farmers' Almanac* handy, you had to look at the height of the sun in the sky and guess. As we drove, we watched the sun drop closer and closer to the horizon. We had guessed wrong.

We were going to miss the sunset.

The sun disappeared below the horizon two minutes before we arrived at the spot, but the sky still heralded glorious shades of pink and yellow. A warm breeze was blowing. We found a spot to spread out our blanket in a sandy, grassy field overlooking the sky's reflection on the water. Tom brought the boom box out.

"I brought some music for us to listen to. Actually, I made a new mixtape for you."

"Oh yeah? What's it called?" I asked, trying to hide the excitement in my voice.

"It's 'Our Story: Part One.'" He hit play. I listened to our story unfold in music. There was a song representing each of our childhoods. And one from our time as just friends. Next, "Somewhere Out There" from *An American Tail*, the movie we'd seen when we first held hands. Then a few more of "our songs" from our seven months of dating.

He stopped the tape deck. "Hey, I forgot something in the car. I'll be right back!" He ran to the car to retrieve this mysterious "something."

My heart was racing. My palms were sweating. Was this it? Was I about to get engaged?

Out of breath, he sat next to me. "And here is 'Our Story: Part Two.'" He pushed the play button on the cassette deck.

The song, "**I Could Never Promise You,**"[1] was new to me. He told me to listen to the words. They were beautiful, and in essence, promised that with God's help, our love for each other would last forever.

As the song ended, Tom clicked the pause button, got on one knee, and asked me to spend the rest of my life with him. Through tears of joy, I said, "Yes!"

Filled with emotion, we gazed at the brilliant Minnesota sky as the light wind rustled the tall grasses around us, and Tom turned on the music again. We listened to "Our Story: Part Three," a compilation of songs about the hopes and dreams we shared. Everything seemed perfect to me, even though we'd missed the sunset.

Which, as it turns out, had been perfect, too. It had given us a great story to tell my parents, aunts, and uncles that brought down the cabin with peals of laughter—a requisite part of every coffee-time story. Tom had passed the test.

I hop on my bike and head toward Barron Lake, a route that's just under nineteen miles. I start at my usual pace, noticing the sun is still a decent distance from the horizon. I spend the first several minutes doing math in my head. *At 12.5 miles per hour, 19 miles should take about an hour and a half. And if the sun sets at 8:16, I probably have until 8:30 before it gets dark, and . . .* My thoughts trail off as I pedal faster.

I don't want to be out on the roads after sunset. Too many bike accidents happen in the dark, either early in the morning or late at night. But do those riders follow all the proper safety precautions? I use a headlight and taillight, wear a helmet, and ride with traffic.

Still, I'm aware none of these safeguards matter if I come up against a distracted driver who veers off the road. I imagine the scenario in my head—the one I've replayed so many times.

I'm hit. Lying on the side of the road. Can I move? Can I reach my phone? Dial 911? Did I catch the license plate number before the driver sped away? Surely someone will see me and come to my rescue. Am I going to survive? Am I going to die?

The sun is nearing the horizon, and so far, I'm not enjoying my ride. I'm focused only on "getting 'er done." As I pass each landmark along the path, I know I'm that much closer to finishing my ride: The busy highway stretch. Done. Beebe Road and the rolling hills. Done. The curve and then the big hill. Done. Four-way stop with a right turn. Done. I'm pedaling hard and so focused on getting home, I don't even notice the pretty farms as I fly by.

The sun seems to taunt me. "I'm gonna' beat you! C'mon, slowpoke!"

I push harder and pass by more landmarks. The elementary school. Check. The lakeside road. Check. The park with the port-a-potty (there's no time for a pit stop today). Check. Crossing the four-lane highway and passing the gas station. Check. Back on the country roads. Check.

I lift my gaze to find the sun. It's almost touching the horizon now. I spot three deer in the grassy fields. On a normal day, I'd stop to watch them, but I've no time tonight. I glance sideways for a second or two as I whiz by and notice wildflowers robed in royal purple and bright, sunshiny yellow. There will be no photo stops this evening. I'm on a mission. Doing the math. *Three miles to go. That's 15 minutes. I should be good. But wait! Maybe there are four miles to go!*

I usually take a break when I ride this far. The only break I have time for now is a quick stop to replace my sunglasses with regular eyeglasses. There's no sun to contend with anymore and it's getting harder to see. The sun has won the race, but I'm coming in a close second.

I make the last turn onto our road as the last remnant of light disappears. Coasting down the driveway, I breathe a sigh of relief. My flashing headlight and tail lights are blinding in the darkness of the garage. I shut them off, hit "pause" on the music, stop tracking my ride on Cyclemeter, and hang my bike on the rack. I'm home.

Our story has unfolded now for over thirty-five years. In the mix-tape of our lives, we're long past "Part Three," having already achieved or sometimes given up on past goals. We've entered mid-life and are passing through at what seems like breakneck speed, with a new bucket list of dreams.

I want to visit all fifty states. Ride a century. Take a photography class. Knit a sweater. Write a book (check!).

Together, we want to take the family on a cruise. Learn ballroom dance. Travel to Italy, Ireland, and Israel; Africa and Asia; return to Greece.

As friends and family who are ahead of us bemoan the fact they're unable to enjoy the activities they used to, we hear our own clocks ticking. The closer we get to those twilight years, the more urgency there is to cross every item off that bucket list.

We make a plan. Determine how many "miles" we have to go and how many years we have left, do the math, and hope we have time to check off every b-list item.

But harried bike rides are a reminder it shouldn't be this way. If we're racing to beat the sunset of our lives, we'll miss it all. Like the beauty of

God's creation around us. Precious moments with loved ones. Tender times we spend together. Laughter and joy.

We'll miss the life we have right here. Right now.

Perhaps it's time to rethink the bucket list. Goals are fine, but if we don't achieve them all before we kick that proverbial bucket, have we failed? Has the journey been a waste of time?

It's wise to plan and hopeful to dream. But we can't stop the sun from setting. Nor can we control every facet of our time on Earth. We don't know what we'll get to do and see before the sun sets on our lives. We've had several dreams, many of which came true as we'd hoped. But others have not.

Our Heavenly Father wrote every day of our stories before we were even born. Along the way there have been plot twists and unexpected turns. Punchlines and paradoxes. Tears of sadness and shouts of joy. Our stories unfold as we live them, not knowing how many pages we have to go, or how our stories will end. That sun is eventually going to set. But racing to beat the sunset steals joy from our ride.

Many years ago, we rushed to see the sunset on the night we got engaged. Missing it was disappointing. Still, we started something beautiful that night on the shores of West Lost Lake; something that continues to this day.

Leaving the story up to our Author-Creator, we already know the perfect ending will come. Instead of rushing to do it all, we can relish in—and give thanks for—the moments we have.

As we journey together, we'll find joy in the ride and at every stop along the way. Joy will show up in the company we keep. And if we pay attention, we'll feel it in the motion and the breeze, we'll hear it in the song, and see it in the light.

If we keep our eyes on the Light and let it shine through our lives, each ride will be a good one, and we'll make it safely home.

TAKE FIVE! QUESTIONS FOR REFLECTION

A Race Against the Sunset: Time to Slow Our Ride

- Recall your engagement story and how it met (or didn't meet) your expectations.

- Do you have a bucket list? How important are those dreams to you?

- How do you practice mindfulness in the moment?

- Can you think of specific ways to enjoy today, rather than live for tomorrow?

- Preserving memories is one way to make the pleasant moments last. How can you preserve memories for yourself and for your children?

A Guide

FROM EMPTY NEST TO MIGHTY NEST

Can we have a roadmap, please?

T om and I have now survived several years without the kids, and we've learned valuable lessons that have transformed our empty nest into a *mighty nest.*

Having kids has brought much joy and happiness, but they changed our lives forever. For years, we cared for, protected, taught, and raised our children. It was an all-consuming, round-the-clock, rewarding-yet-tiresome job.

During twenty-six years of (at-home) parenting, there were many times we looked at each other wistfully and said, "Remember when it was just the two of us?" But as I gave our youngest child a tight, tearful, goodbye hug on her college move-in day, I wondered, *Are we prepared for this? Are we going to remember how to be "just the two of us?"*

The unfamiliar empty-nest life stage can bring on anxiety, fear, and excitement all at once. It's disorienting as, once again, our lives change.

The term "empty" refers to the absence of something. Like an empty gas tank, fridge, or wine glass, emptiness is typically undesirable. An empty home brings to mind a sad, lonely place.

But when I switched my license plate from "KID MVR" to "MTY NST" and realized "MTY" looked more like "Mighty" than the "Empty" I'd intended it to represent, I began to view this life stage in a whole new light.

When I thought of our nest as being mighty rather than empty, I could see a plethora of benefits such as strength, possibility, freedom, and hope!

Sure, there've been bumps along the way and Tom and I are still a work in progress, but we've also found a roadmap that offers us a smoother path on which we can experience our *Empty-Nest Joyride*. May it do the same for you.

A Roadmap from Empty Nest to Mighty Nest

M - Mingle Moments and Amusements
I - Ignite Individual Interests
G - Get Together with God
H - Hang with your Homies
T - Travel Together
Y - Yak with the Young'uns
N - Notice Neighbors in Need
E - Exercise and Eat Right
S - Simply Simplify
T - Take Time to Reflect and Give Thanks

M: Mingle Moments and Amusements

The mighty-nest years have come with a newfound freedom, unfilled blocks of time, and more togetherness in marriage. It wasn't too long ago that our lives followed a distinctly different pattern.

During the early parenting years, our activities and excitement revolved around little people. Together, Tom and I watched each baby discover the world. We laughed at their antics and celebrated their achievements. We photographed and videotaped every adorable expression and miraculous feat.

"Look how he puckers when he eats applesauce!"

"He loves peek-a-boo!"

"Listen to her 'read' her favorite book!"

"Watch her dance when I turn on 'Barney!'"

Friends and family smiled at these stories and photos, but no one enjoyed them as much as we did.

Then came the school years. Our calendar was packed year-round. We immersed ourselves in the children.

But the advent of our mighty-nest era changed all that. When the social calendar became ours to do with as we wished, we filled it with amusements we both enjoy.

With the freedom of our mighty nest and a little more discretionary spending money, we often attend a local university's productions, or catch plays and musicals at the civic theater nearby. If we're in a "spendy" mood, we splurge on an off-Broadway show locally or in Chicago—the nearest big city.

We occasionally attend concerts of some of our favorite artists, like Jack Johnson and Billy Joel. It sparks joy and romance as we sway to the music we love today or sing along to the tunes from younger years.

Tom loves watching sports, both in person and on TV. We both love the fanfare and excitement of a tailgater and football game at Notre Dame, our local university. For Christmas, I stuff his stocking with pairs of tickets to local basketball or hockey games. He enjoys watching the competition while I revel in the activities and music surrounding them.

One of our favorite pastimes is visiting wineries near home. Their hillside vineyards are a picturesque backdrop year-round as the winemakers explain their processes and we sip their carefully crafted whites and reds.

Of course, we're also fond of biking. When we explore new trails, we connect with each other and with God's creation. The organized rides on summer weekends offer a change of scenery and the camaraderie of other bikers.

Other mutually enjoyable activities include fishing, kayaking, or playing online games like Wordle and Connections. Whatever we're engaged in, we're fortunate we both love several of the same activities, allowing us to "mingle our moments." Still, it helps to be intentional about time we spend together.

Brainstorm with your partner to find activities that captivate you both. Then pursue those activities and *mingle your moments and amusements!*

I: Ignite Individual Interests

J ust as time spent together is crucial, so is time spent alone in personal pursuits. Having a mighty nest allows us the opportunity to ignite individual interests, since we now have more time and energy to engage in them. I encourage Tom to be the best he can be, and I'm thankful he does the same for me. Keeping each other's zest and passions alive results in a fulfilling life, bringing out the best in each of us.

But after years of putting kids first, I'm discovering that some of my earlier personal interests no longer thrill me—things such as shopping and fashion, sewing and counted cross-stitch.

However, I still love scrapbooking, albeit the digital variety these days. When our babies were young, I spent hours at scrapbooking parties with friends or family, where we shared photos and kid stories while supporting each other through motherhood.

Knitting, a skill I learned during the kids' school-aged years, has become my textile art of choice. It's relaxing, and the finished product is something I'm often able to gift or use myself. It also allows me to stream a favorite TV show while still feeling productive.

I read more now than I did when my nest was full. Besides setting yearly reading goals (and tracking them online), I follow many writers on Substack, which is a cross between a blog and a social media site. I also enjoy listening to podcasts to further expand my knowledge of the world.

The most surprising interest I've discovered in my mighty-nest journey is writing. I'd dabbled in it before, but it was only after some online instruction and lots of practice that my love for writing grew, which has led to my blog and Substack newsletter, freelance opportunities, and even publishing books!

As for my better half, it often seems Tom is ignoring me. I get frustrated until I realize he can't hear me because he's wearing his AirPods to listen to podcasts, audiobooks, and Spotify playlists. He's an avid playlist maker, so I often steal them for my enjoyment. He also enjoys challenging games and puzzles that keep his brain sharp. His primary activity, though, is moving. Whether cycling, walking, or working on his honey-do list around the yard or house, he likes to move.

Think about the dreams you've put on hold or that hobby you never had time for when parenting. You may no longer be tuned in to what your passions are.

Here are some good questions to start with:

During your parenting years, what part of yourself was yearning to be set free? Who are you now and what do you love to do? Or, who *were* you and what *did* you love before becoming a parent?

Don't give up on your goals. The mighty-nest years are the perfect time to dust them off and achieve them!

G: Get Together with God

L ike red hair, green eyes, and Dutch blood, my faith is a part of me. Parents and grandparents passed their faith down to me, teaching me to say prayers at mealtimes and bedtime as soon as I could talk. When I could read, they gave me a Bible. I learned to sing and harmonize standing between my mom and sister in church, as they belted out hymns in their strong alto voices.

My beliefs grew along with me, as did Tom's. On our wedding day, Tom and I promised to keep Christ as the foundation of our marriage. When we had our children baptized, we promised to instruct them in the faith.

For years, family devotion time after dinner focused on teaching the kids basic tenets of faith; the beliefs central to our lives. As we tucked them in at night, we memorized prayers with them. While the nest was full, my time with God was largely time with God *and* family.

My one-on-one time with God often faltered during those years. Though I joined the occasional Bible study, I didn't always engage in personal devotions due to the busyness of working nearly full time and meeting the family's needs. I knew God would have been happy with five minutes spent in his Word each day, but there were many days when even that didn't happen.

Still, God held onto me. I prayed and spent time in weekly worship. I turned to him as a source of comfort and strength during difficult times. God was patient, and when the nest finally emptied, he gently called me back. I could no longer blame lack of time for my lack of personal devotions. I again joined a Bible study and spent more time in his word, and I began to share my faith through writing.

Tom and I have also become more intentional in sharing our faith as a couple. Tom's Sunday morning playlists kick off each week with a spiritual mindset as choral or contemporary worship music fills our home and hearts. We read devotional books, seasonal reflections about Advent and Lent, and books of the Bible that our congregational family studies together. Time spent with a small group from church has also helped us grow in faith.

While we sometimes falter in this habit, we strive to hold each other accountable in our spiritual lives. When we fall behind or get into a pattern of sameness that no longer inspires, we know it's time to look wider and dig deeper in our relationship with God.

If you've been falling behind in your spiritual journey, or have gotten into a rut of distractions or practices that no longer inspire you, let your mighty-nest years encourage you to *get together with God* in richer, more meaningful ways.

H: Hang with your Homies

L ike planets revolving around the sun, nearly every aspect of our lives—entertainment; sleep, eat, and work schedules; finances; and social activities—revolve around children when they live under our roofs. Kids have a way of shrinking the universe in that way.

But kids also have a way of expanding our universe! Many of Tom's and my dearest friends are those we met because of the kids—friends who walked side-by-side with us through the parenting years.

We bonded with them in the stands at soccer games and marching band competitions. We ate ice cream sundaes at Dairy Queen together after concerts and Christmas programs. And when the high-school thespians piled their shoes a mile high at the doorstep and descended into our basement for their cast party, a gratified bunch of theater parents joined us upstairs for a well-deserved glass of wine.

All of them identified with our parenting struggles—sleepless nights, sick kids, tumultuous teenagers. Thank goodness they were there to listen and offer advice! But then it was all over. The kids were gone. The activities halted. And our social lives took a nosedive.

Although it's tempting to stay home on those free weekend nights and go to bed early (since we finally can!), we know being total homebodies is not healthy for us. So, we often reach out to the homies—our friends and family—and hang out with them over coffee, dinner, or drinks. There's something to be treasured in every friend, regardless of the age or stage of life.

Friends of similar ages celebrate with us in our newfound freedom, and we trade stories on the latest happenings of each young adult child. We draw upon the experiences of retired friends as we deal with young adult struggles and we're inspired as we watch them fulfill their retirement dreams. Friends with younger children keep us young (and grateful we're past those stages!) as they seek our advice. (We like to think they consider us to be the "wise ones.")

Our "homies" also include extended families. Spending time with and caring for aging parents is priceless and often necessary. Weekends with my sisters, a tradition that started when our kids were young, now occurs without the worry of kid schedules or the guilt of leaving home for a couple of days.

Who are your "homies"? Colleagues from work? Friends or a "small group" from your church? Your neighbors? Extended family?

Plan on spending more time deepening those relationships once your kids have flown the nest. *Hanging with your homies* will make life sweet and satisfying.

T: Travel Together

You've probably seen the Dr. Seuss book, *Oh, the Places You'll Go!* Perhaps you've given it or received it as a baby shower or graduation gift. Personally, I think it would make a great empty-nester gift for those of us embarking on a grand new adventure. We're finally free to go!

Tom and I occasionally got away when the kids were young, but the planning and preparation it required often prevented us from traveling on a whim. And with the vacation budget spent on trips for the whole family, there wasn't much left for a couple-only getaway.

Enter the mighty-nest years. We're no longer tied down to kids' care or schedules. Plus, we now have kids living in four different states, which gives us at least a few good excuses to travel.

During that first year as mighty nesters, we spent a week reuniting with long-time friends from college at a beach house on the East Coast and celebrated our thirtieth anniversary with an amazing trip to Mexico. With the sound of waves crashing against the shore, lulling us to sleep at night, it was the perfect location for a romantic celebration of thirty years of marriage.

Planning getaways involves determining where and when to go, figuring out a budget, and booking hotels or rental homes. It requires us to work together as a couple at compromising and decision making. But this work is a pleasure when dreaming of vacation destinations!

Depending on the type of vacation, you can easily build in your other mighty-nest habits, including mingling moments together, igniting individual interests, getting together with God, and hanging with friends or family.

Although we're empty nesters now, we love it when the kids can vacation with us. We've extended a standing invitation for them to join us during our time at the lakeshore cabin in Minnesota. But the busier they get with their own lives, the harder it is to get the gang together. We take what we can get, and when all the stars align, we relish vacation times with the whole family.

Where do you want to travel? Are there short weekend trips you could make? Or are you ready to take that cruise or overseas vacation of your dreams? What's holding you back?

"Today is your day! You're off to Great Places! You're off and away! Oh, the places you'll go!" (Dr. Seuss, 1990,)[1]

Y: Yak with the Young'uns

Today's kids can call, text, Snapchat, message, FaceTime or video chat with their parents anytime, day or night. And ours do!

Compare that to when I left for college. My parents gave me permission to call them once a week (unless, of course, there was an emergency). I was to "call collect" on Sunday afternoons, so they could refuse the call and then call me back on their dime, which was also the cheapest option.

When our kids moved off to college, we received many calls and texts, often accompanied by tears or crying emojis as they poured out their latest academic, health, or relationship crises. Later, as they entered the learning-to-adult years, they called seeking advice on taxes, insurance, jobs, housing, or to get a favorite recipe.

Yet the longer they were away from the nest, the less they needed us. Not hearing from them sometimes caused me to feel lonely or sad, but hadn't we always hoped they'd one day find their way in the world?

I came to realize that their independence shouldn't mean a lost connection with them. Rather than always waiting for the kids to call us, we try to make a point of calling them (or reminding them to call us).

Our communication is more about connecting than problem solving. We love to hear from them, even when—especially when—everything is going well. We enjoy catching up with them, hearing of their latest exploits, and filling our home with the sounds of their voices again. We still give plenty of (unsolicited) advice, but these chats focus more on "how have you been?" and "what's new?"

Whole-family conversations are also important. Snapchats, Instagram posts, and text messages are nice for keeping tabs on each other, but it's even better to set up a time to call or video chat and put it on the calendar, like any other meeting. Finding a time when we're all available to chat without feeling rushed allows the conversations to go deeper, beyond the quick surface information.

The kids may no longer be in our nest, but they'll forever be on our minds and in our hearts. And the love we share across the miles, through fiber-optic connections and light-speed synapses, is a reminder of how full and blessed our mighty nest still is.

How do you keep in touch with your kids? Do you reach out to them, or depend on them to contact you? If you have multiple kids, grandkids, etc., have you considered scheduling a group video chat?

Consider your children's needs, schedules, and options for communicating, and make *yakking with your young 'uns* a goal today!

N: Notice Neighbors in Need

Tom's love language is "acts of service." We took the "love languages" quiz early on, and as the recipient of his acts of service for over three decades now, I can attest it's true.

He soon learned I'm not a morning person and that I need coffee to get me going. He also drinks coffee, so he gets up every morning (almost without fail) to make us a fresh pot of coffee. Not only that, he delivers it to me at my bedside table, my bathroom vanity, or wherever he finds me. This is a prime example of the love language he speaks.

But his acts of service don't stop with me. He's the one showing up for church clean-up days, helping countless people move, and packing or distributing boxes for the big "food drop" in our community. For a couple of years after the kids left home, he gave up his lunch hour one day a week to read with struggling readers at a local elementary school.

"Acts of service" is *not* my love language, but it's something I know I *should* do, *want* to do, and—when I take the time to do it—am *blessed* by doing.

With more time as mighty nesters, we look for opportunities to notice neighbors in need. One year, I challenged myself to do an act of service each month. Through volunteering at a community center Christmas shop, helping with a food drive, and giving blood, there were ample opportunities to serve. Although I didn't meet my annual goal, helping others through the service projects I took part in was fulfilling.

When I look around me, I see plenty of people in need. Some kids I work with come to school in the winter without decent coats and boots. Taking the time to go through our kids' outgrown winter things and bringing them directly to school has been a meaningful use of my time.

Our church offers plenty of opportunities for service, including taking meals to fellow church members after an illness, injury, or birth of a new baby. It's so gratifying to see the look of appreciation in a young couple's eyes as you deliver the meal to their doorstep, days after they bring a newborn home. A bonus is that I usually get my baby fix by holding the precious little one for a few minutes.

Tom and I once said someday we'd like to join a mission trip. Even though it hasn't yet fit into our lives, there have been plenty of opportunities to do missional work in our own backyard. All it takes is the motivation to seek out a project or service, sign up, and show up.

Are you currently noticing your neighbors in need? Consider how you can give of your time, talents, and treasure to help others. It'll bring dividends you never expected.

E: Exercise and Eat Right

Despite my pleasingly plump body, I aim to be as healthy as possible, which no longer equates to fitting into my "skinny jeans."

I've never had an athletic or slim figure. Along with red hair, I also inherited the genetic disposition for being heavy. My extra pounds have plagued me, annoyed me, and—when I was younger—left me in tears. I've been on diets and I've lost weight, but it usually finds me again.

Over the years, I've learned that being healthy simply means feeling good and maintaining a healthy lifestyle. The longer Tom and I can do that, the more activities and enjoyment we hope to experience in our later years.

While our mighty nest affords us more time for exercise, staying motivated continues to be a challenge for me. As my body ages, I'm learning the value of a variety of physical activities. Fitness watches, habit trackers, and accountability partners have been important tools on my journey. They keep me walking, riding, kayaking, stretching, working out, and doing yoga.

Another key to a healthy lifestyle is eating right. But knowing what's "right" can be confusing. I'm not an expert or dietician, but I've read enough diet plans and studied enough healthy eating recommendations to know many of the trends and tips contradict each other. One study says to cut fat and eat all veggies and grains. Another says cut the carbs and pile on protein, healthy fat, and veggies.

Tom and I have attempted several diet plans over the years. Because of my specific family history, I keep coming back to the practical guidelines of the DASH and MIND diets as good general rules of thumb. Tracking my food intake on apps like My Fitness Pal or Weight Watchers has helped me regain control when I've fallen off the healthy eating wagon.

Since becoming mighty nesters, we've exercised more and have eaten healthier meals. Are we the model for eating right and working out? Definitely not. Do I think we could (and should) do better? You bet.

Sometimes we take baby steps toward a healthier lifestyle. At other times, we take giant leaps. When bodies rebel through pain, discomfort, or fatigue, we know it's time to make our physical selves a priority again. When we do, it feels good to eat well and move more.

How have you incorporated healthy habits into your empty-nest life? Are there ways you could improve your health and fitness? If so, try adding one healthy habit (or subtracting an unhealthy one), on your journey to better health today!

S: Simply Simplify

There's an "empty-box mountain" in our attic. Boxes that our electronics came packaged in. American Girl doll and Lego boxes. Amazon boxes. Once every year or so, I go through them and pitch a bunch. But before long, the mountain grows again. I often wonder why I keep them.

Shortly after we became empty nesters, I bought the book, *The Life-Changing Magic of Tidying Up* by Marie Kondo. We used her method to declutter much of our home, and it truly did "spark some joy." I wouldn't call it life changing, but it did change the atmosphere in the house to one of less clutter and more simplicity.

We began eliminating items by donating or selling things online. We sorted through hundreds of books, and purged ourselves of four or five boxes full of them. I decluttered the kitchen cabinets by removing unused cups, vases, and trays. Tom untangled a jungle of cords we'd accumulated from old computers, cameras, and phones. We went through our closets and dresser drawers and filled several bags with clothes and shoes that we delivered to the local Goodwill store. With each room we tackled, a weight was lifted.

But the job of decluttering is never finished. Once you finally get through every area, it's time to start over again.

We've learned that *simplifying* is not only getting rid of extra items that drag us down, but it's also consuming less. The more we buy, the more we have to care for, clean, repair, and eventually eliminate. If we're more discerning in our purchases—waiting until we need (rather than want) new clothes, or using small appliances until they die instead of replacing them because a newer, shinier model is on sale—then consumption decreases.

All of this goes hand-in-hand with a Swedish trend called "death-cleaning." The concept is to reduce the number of possessions you have before you die so you don't burden your children with the task of sorting through and getting rid of things.

The children will be much happier if you've already eliminated unimportant items and kept only sentimental treasures. Keep the items that continue to spark joy for you or will bring joy to your children as they remember you through them.

The mighty-nest years are a great time to simplify as you look toward the future. At some point, you may want to downsize. The thought of moving all that stuff might be overwhelming, but the more you remove now, the less you'll need to worry about later.

Tom and I periodically go through the motions of simplifying, but I'm still growing that "empty-box mountain" in the attic. Maybe they'll come in handy for hauling more "treasures" to Goodwill, sending a package now and then, or moving to a smaller home someday.

Do you want to simplify your life? Not sure how or where to start? Look around your home and pick one cluttered area to begin with. There are many guides available to help you through the process. Then, grab a box or garbage bag and start pitching!

T: Take Time to Reflect and Give Thanks

As I look back at how quickly our parenting years flew by, I'm reminded of the saying, "Don't blink." Now I see the wisdom in that advice, but back then I didn't have time to think about it.

We simply went through the motions of such mindless tasks as laundry, baths, meals, and housecleaning. I must have blinked often because the details of all those years are fuzzy, if I can remember them at all.

Our human perceptions of time are interesting. While we wait for a big event like a wedding day, the birth of a baby, or a ride at Disney World, time seems to drag. It's as if someone has slowed down the spin of the earth as we wait for the minutes and days to pass.

Looking back on the event afterward, however, the experience itself seems to have flown by, as if someone gave the globe a good twirl to get it spinning rapidly again. The roller coaster you waited two hours for lasted only thirty seconds, the baby you waited nine months for was born in (hopefully) a few hours, and the wedding you dreamed of for years was over in a day.

During momentous occasions, emotions are fully engaged, which often increases our ability to remember them. Memories, like scrapbooks, allow us to revisit those events—to view them in the mind's eye—to make them last.

Life can slip away if we let it, so I've started "not blinking" more often, through mindfulness. I pay attention not only to the people and events in my life but also to the backdrop of God's creation—from mighty mountains to minuscule miracles, like snowflakes and honeybees. Mindfulness requires me to stop and notice not only my surroundings, but also associated thoughts and feelings. In doing so, I call on God's hand to touch that rapidly spinning globe ever so gently—to slow my thoughts so I can attend to these ordinary, yet extraordinary, blessings.

In my experience, one outcome of mindfulness is thankfulness. For a time, I kept a gratitude journal. At the end of each day, I listed five things for which I was thankful. On busy days, I'd often resort to no-brainers like "family" or "a loving husband." But on days when I had time to be mindful—to keep my eyes wide open—I listed details like a flag dancing in the wind, the sun reflecting on a puddle, holes in Swiss cheese, and the invention of the automobile. I included every little thing. Every big thing. And everything in between.

Another practice that has turned my mindfulness into thankfulness is a "daily examen." Lying in bed at night, I recall three ways God has shown up for me that day. Recalling his presence—often through others in my life—nearly always brings me a sense of peace and gratitude. But being mindful can also increase awareness of pain—both my own and that of others. Confrontation, illness, heartbreak, and loss are all inevitable in this life.

Reflecting on the goodness *and* brokenness in the world reminds me of a phrase I heard once in a sermon: "We're on our way, but we're not there yet."

It's like being in the middle of a bike ride—I experience joy from the wind on my face and the beauty of creation all around, but then feel a twinge of pain in my back or see a pile of trash littering the roadside. Still, I keep moving, knowing my destination promises the rest and comfort I long for, but also realizing the joy of this ride will end when I get there.

I'm on my way, but I'm not there yet.

How can you pay attention to the road you're on as well as your destination? Can you reflect the beauty of the "not yet" into your "now?"

By slowing down and being grateful in the moment, and by trusting in the One on whose promises we can depend, our ride will get us through each day and take us to that ultimate joy-filled destination.

Acknowledgements

This book would not have been possible without the unending support, guidance, and encouragement of my companions on the journey. Some, with their expertise, literally left their imprint on the pages. Others, though not directly part of the book's publishing, have lives so inextricably woven into my story, that I can't imagine taking this ride without them.

To all of you, my deepest, heartfelt thanks.

To God, " [Who] can do anything, you know—far more than you could ever imagine or guess or request in your wildest dreams! He does it not by pushing us around but by working within us, his Spirit deeply and gently within us." (Eph. 3:20, MSG). Thank you, Lord, for working gently within me to accomplish this work that I surely didn't imagine thirty-some years ago.

To Tom, you've given me the ride of my life! Having you by my side—as we raised our beautiful, busy family, and now as we slow down and enjoy our quiet but mighty nest—is truly a gift. Thank you for believing in and encouraging my book dream. Thank you for pumping up my tires, bringing me coffee in the morning, and keeping the spark in our marriage alive.

To my children: Jared, Seth and Maddie, Leah and Garrett, and Chloe; you have filled the pages of my life with laughter and tears, adventures and challenges, but most of all, with joy. Thank you for all you've taught and continue to teach me. *And to my grandchildren,* I pray you bring as much joy to your parents as they have brought to me. (But throw in a little mischief for good measure. After all, it's payback time!)

To my sisters—by blood or marriage—Phyllis, Barb, Beth, Diane, and Beth K; you've been my steady companions on this journey. Thank you for teaching me the importance of family, whether we're together or apart. And thanks for cheering me on in this crazy midlife adventure!

To my parents, Harold and Eleanor, and Tom's parents, Dave and Joyce—whom I wish were still with us so I could thank in person; you have all given Tom and me the greatest examples of love and commitment in marriage. Thank you for the love you shared with each other, and that you showered on us and our children.

To Mary V.K. and Cheryl Balcom, my pre-readers who found the gaps, but mostly reassured me of the value of sharing my stories with others. And *to Linda Cobourn*—the faithful member/leader of our critique group—for your writerly insight, instruction, and invitation to show up month after month, for years.

To Dalene Bickel, editor extraordinaire. Thanks for helping me polish my work with minimal harm to "my darlings." *To Madalyn H.,* for sharing your hidden talent for proofreading and attention to detail. *To Scott D.*, for your time, keen eye, and way with words.

To Ruthie Gray and my "treasured team." Thank you for getting me back in the saddle so I could clear the clutter and clarify the path to the book-pub finish line. And *to Callie Feyen,* for setting me on that path over six years ago.

To my Substack community. Thank you for letting me drop in your inbox week after week; for reading, commenting, "hitting the heart," and giving me the confidence to keep writing.

To you, my generous reader. Thank you for taking this *Joyride* with me. Wherever you are on your journey, I hope my words have enriched your life and enabled you to find *hope, love, and purpose—together with joy—on the road to contentment.*

Endnotes

The (Re)Construction Zone

1. Michael Franti & Spearhead, "**Life is Better with You**," *All People* (Capital Records, 2013).

Winter Training

1. John Guarnieri, Nehemiah Persoff, and Warren Hays, "There Are No Cats In America," (*An American Tale*, 1986).

2. Linda Ronstadt and James Ingram, "**Somewhere, Out There**," (*An American Tale*, 1986).

The Rhythm of the Ride

1. Andy Grammer, "**Good To Be Alive (Hallelujah),**" *Magazines or Novels* (S-Curve Records, 2015).

2. Phillip Phillips, "**Home**," *The World from the Side of the Moon* (Interscope, 2012).

3. Led Zeppelin, "**Stairway to Heaven**," *Led Zeppelin IV* (Atlantic, 1971).

4. Owl City feat. Aloe Blacc, "**Verge**," *Mobile Orchestra*, (Republic, 2015).

5. Zac Brown Band, "**I Play the Road**," *You Get What You Give*, (Keith Stegall & Zac Brown, 2010).

6. Big Daddy Weave, "**Audience of One**," *One and Only* (Word Entertainment LLC, a Curb Company, 2002).

Fears and What-ifs

1. Ben Fielding and Reuben Morgan, "Mighty to Save," *Mighty to Save,* (Hillsong Music Australia, 2006).

2. Jerry Bock and Sheldon Harnick, "Matchmaker, Matchmaker," (*Fiddler on the Roof*, 1964).

3. Jerry Bock and Sheldon Harnick, "**Sabbath Prayer**," (*Fiddler on the Roof*, 1964).

4. Jerry Bock and Sheldon Harnick, "**Sunrise, Sunset**," (*Fiddler on the Roof*, 1964).

Against the Wind

1. Lionel Bart, "It's a Fine Life," (*Oliver!* 1960).

The Trike

1. Lori McKenna, "**People Get Old**," *The Tree* (Thirty Tigers, 2018).

Going the Distance

1. Harry Connick, Jr. "**(I Do) Like We Do**," *That Would Be Me* (Columbia, 2015).

A Race Against the Sunset

1. Don Francisco, "**I Could Never Promise You**," *The Live Concert* (NewPax, 1982).

T: Travel Together

1. Dr. Seuss, *Oh, The Places You'll Go!*. New York: Random House, 1990.

About the author

Linda Hanstra, a semi-retired speech-language pathologist, is living happily ever after-the-kids with her husband, Tom, in southwest Michigan. They spend summers at the lake in northern Minnesota—their home away from home.

On quiet evenings and summer afternoons, you might find her reading, knitting, cycling, or kayaking. As a mother of four, and now "Lala" too, her family and faith bring her the deepest joy. The author of *Lent through the Little Things: Encountering Jesus in Life's Ordinary Moments,* Linda has been blogging and sharing encouragement for couples, parents, and empty nesters for over ten years.

You can connect with Linda on Instagram, Facebook, Substack, and on her website: www.lindahanstra.com.

FOR MORE EMPTY-NEST ENCOURAGEMENT, HOP ON "THE JOYRIDE"

Linda has been encouraging readers for over ten years through stories of *faith, family, empty nesting, cycling, travel, lake life*, and more, on Substack and at LindaHanstra.com.

Subscribe to receive her newsletter (2-4 times/month) and *get stories, links, and other updates* delivered right to your inbox!

Hop On!

DID YOU ENJOY THE RIDE?

If so, *please* help others find this book
by leaving a *rating and/or review!*

Empty-Nest Joyride
on Amazon:

Empty-Nest Joyride
on Goodreads:

Thank you for supporting an independent author!

ALSO BY LINDA HANSTRA

A 40-day Lenten devotional to help you encounter Jesus in your everyday moments and surroundings—at the shoe store, the kitchen sink, a coffee shop, or in your car.

God leaves his mark on all creation, if only we look for him. These readings will bring you to the cross, where the Savior offers free and abundant grace!

www.ingramcontent.com/pod-product-compliance
Lightning Source LLC
Chambersburg PA
CBHW061731120626

46550CB00005B/1771

9789898766612 8